Praise for
Things My Mama Told Me

"Olga Samples Davis embodies the precious gift of embrace. Her gracious writing invites us to sit on the porch right alongside her, delighting in the wit and wisdom springing up from the deep, compassionate mama-well. She's terrific at writing conversations and including the buzzes of friction that spark larger understanding. I wish she and her mama ran the world."

—NAOMI SHIHAB NYE, author of *Habibi*

"In this book, you will find the wisdom of a strong, vibrant, and free-spirited mother, who shaped not only the lives of her children but her extended family and community as well.… In *Things My Mama Told Me,* a devoted and endearing daughter puts her mother's heart of mountain-moving wisdom on delightful display."

—THELMA WELLS, singer, speaker, and author
of *Girl, Have I Got News for You*

"Olga is opening her great heart, sharp mind, and witty wisdom for the world. It is the down-to-earth wisdom presented with mercy and mirth that feeds some deep yearning in all of our hearts. Readers will…wish that they could sit down with this playfully wise woman and her mom, Browning, and have all day to simply talk about the things that really matter in life."

—DON MURDOCK, executive director of Laity Lodge,
H. E. Butt Foundation, and marriage and family therapist

"*Things My Mama Told Me* could be read in a day, but it will take a lifetime to adequately use and fully enjoy. Here's one sure way mamas of old can inspire mamas (and daddies) of today. Through writing that is both refreshing and aspiring, Olga gives us clues to their rearing genius. It's like a guide for today's parents—easy to follow and fun to read."

— GEMERAL E. BERRY JR., journalist and publisher
    of *Our Texas* magazine

"Many of us are blessed to have mothers like Browning Louvenia McKinney Samples, whose boundless love, life-affirming spirit, and poetic pearls of wisdom have nurtured and shaped us. But few of our mothers are blessed enough to have children like Olga Samples Davis who are equally poetic and wise in articulating our mother's teachings. After you've finished reading *Things My Mama Told Me,* you may not be as wise as Browning and Olga, but I promise that you will be wiser, better, more inspired, and more in love with life and appreciative of its wonders than you were before you opened it."

— CARY CLACK, columnist, *San Antonio Express-News*

"*Things My Mama Told Me* is a glorious collection of proverbs and family stories from a remarkable mother who gave her children joy, beauty, self-reliance, hope, and the power of God. The mighty partnership of mother-love and the Almighty issues from these pages in nothing less than abracadabra thunderbolts. Dip in, read, and ponder, then share with your mother or daughter. What a feast."

— ELLEN SHULL, editor of *Palo Alto Review,* professor of English

"Creative, provocative, energetic, and direct in the storytelling approach, Olga Samples Davis captures the interest and inner spirit of the reader as she shows lessons learned while offering moral lessons. This book is refreshing and will serve as a wonderful guide for mothers and daughters in their efforts to show love, strength, determination, success, and survival."

—ANGIE S. RUNNELS, PHD, college president, lecturer,
and mother

"A beautifully written, funny, moving, and inspiring look at a mother-daughter relationship that spans decades. This book is sure to bring women a renewed perspective of our biblical calling to pass on true treasure to another generation."

—ANDI ASHWORTH, author of *Real Love for Real Life*

"Olga's wit and wonderful storytelling embody the full spectrum of her mother's wisdom, giving this book the capacity to pierce our minds, hearts, and spirits with priceless God-centered values for life."

—BITSY AYRES RUBSAMEN, author of *Gentle Rain*
and *Becoming the Beloved*

"The eloquence of Professor Olga Samples Davis speaks volumes about the possibilities of causing language to become words of life. This collection of poems and stories is an odyssey describing how we all can journey from the trials of childhood to the triumph of maturity, regardless of our age."

—CIRO D. RODRIGUEZ, U.S. representative from Texas

Things My

MAMA
TOLD
ME

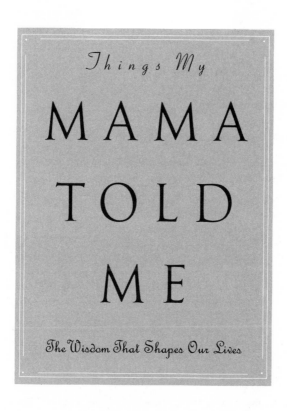

Things My

MAMA

TOLD

ME

The Wisdom That Shapes Our Lives

OLGA SAMPLES DAVIS

WATERBROOK
PRESS

THINGS MY MAMA TOLD ME
PUBLISHED BY WATERBROOK PRESS
2375 Telstar Drive, Suite 160
Colorado Springs, Colorado 80920
A division of Random House, Inc.

Details in some anecdotes and stories have been changed to protect the identities
of the persons involved.

ISBN 1-57856-819-6

Library of Congress Cataloging-in-Publication Data
Davis, Olga Samples.
  Things my mama told me : the wisdom that shapes our lives / Olga Samples
Davis.— 1st ed.
      p. cm.
Includes bibliographical references.
  ISBN 1-57856-819-6
 1. Christian life—Anecdotes. 2. Christian life—Meditations. I. Title.
  BV4501.3.D38 2004
  248.4—dc22

                                    2003026029

Printed in the United States of America
2004—First Edition

10 9 8 7 6 5 4 3 2 1

For Clinton Davis

whose sweet love, spirit,
and phenomenal courage
lives beyond
ashes and oceans

CONTENTS

MY MOTHER, MY FRIEND

I do not know how long I had been staring in admiration at my mother. She was fast approaching her eightieth birthday, and she looked better than I did. As an observer, I had always enjoyed watching Mama's spirit of adventure soar as she anticipated travel to some old or new land—or dared to try new things. As a learner, I was so grateful to have inherited some of her "let's try something different" sass. She could be excited about so many simple things most of us take for granted and see playful mischief as an ally when she wanted your attention.

It was not uncommon when Mama and I traveled together to find ourselves finishing each other's sentences—or simply driving along silently in full conversation. Treasured moments with a Mother-friend. How many times had I heard Mama say, "One day, if you're lucky, your children will also become your friends"? *We are definitely a lucky pair,* I thought as we piled into the car and set out to do something new.

She spied an object on the seat. "What is this?" she asked.

I laughed as I announced, "This is a compass, given to me by an angel of a friend who said she wanted me to be able to find my way when I am lost."

Mama chuckled as I handed her my instrument guide. "You will need more than a compass to help you find your way in this world!"

Accept it, I said to myself. *You are her target today.*

"And for those of us who really know you," Mama continued, "we have come to accept that you often can't find your way out of a paper bag."

Shared laughter shook our bodies. It wasn't what she said as much as how she said it. But she was right about finding our way in the world. Even with direction, we need more. A suitcase of discipline, work, kindness, and perseverance are requirements. A backpack of love, faith, history, heritage, hope, and humor are absolute necessities. And it also helps to be pointed in the right direction. These are just some of the things my mama has given me over the past fifty-five years since I, her second child, was born.

Long before the phrase "shock and awe" was coined, I experienced it firsthand with my mama—a five-foot-three-inch-one-hundred-twenty-five-pound-soaking-wet spitfire and I-shall-not-be-moved-spirit force of faith, courage, character, and earthshaking love. The third of six children born to the Reverend Carson Robert and Louvenia Ward McKinney, Browning Anna Louvenia McKinney insists it is important to note that on the day of her birth in Huntsville, Texas, a prisoner from the state penitentiary escaped and bloodhounds surrounded the house with melodic howls—welcoming her arrival to the world.

Always fiercely independent and responsible, Browning held a job at an early age to help support her family. After graduating from high school, she left home to go to barber college, then settled in the "big city" of San Antonio, Texas. There she met Eugene Oneida Samples, my father. "Gene" owned the building that housed the barbershop where Browning was employed. When he sat in her barber chair, his intention was to give this newcomer an opportunity to establish herself in an all-male shop by cutting his hair. A few months later the Bunyan-built man realized that this dark-skinned, sapphire-jeweled woman was far more than a professional barber—she should be his wife. The courtship was serious and brief. After they married, stairstepped children followed.

My sister, Carlotta, premiered. I came next, followed by my brother, Ronald. Growing up in our barn of a house with high ceilings, wooden floors, and a sun porch crowded with exotic plants and flowers was an adventure in delight and discovery. Growing up in our community was a commitment to weekly library visits, field trips, studying, and volunteerism. Growing up in our church meant all-day Sunday affairs with weekday choir and junior usher board rehearsals. Growing up with Daddy Gene was to witness the diverse parade of humanity that found its way to the Zumbro—his barbershop, restaurant, and hotel complex where people of color found a safe haven of good food and rest for their weary souls.

Daddy died when we were six, five, and four, respectively. How well I remember the day of Daddy's funeral…hiding under the dining room table and listening to strangers and kinfolk talk doom and gloom about our future. I thought, *You don't know my mama!* True to form, Mama exhibited amazing grace. As monetary and emotional crises loomed, her Christian faith prevailed and soared. To look at her was to be assured that we would not drown in a sea of problems even when a vortex of grief, confusion, despair, and indecision threatened. Only in retrospect did I understand how fortunate I was to be the child of two incredibly strong parents with attitudes and actions that declared, "Bring this life thing on, because I am ready for whatever comes my way!"

Those next few years without Daddy were filled with challenges. Mama managed our home, school, community, and extracurricular responsibilities as she worked odd jobs, kept the Zumbro alive, and tried to get the business sold. Often I found her asleep in a den chair or at the kitchen table, too tired to find her bed. I lived in awe of her determination to use so many of her waking hours to help us improve our lives as individuals and as members of the human family.

After our promotion to middle school, Mama continued working while she went back to college to earn a degree in education. Soon after this decision, our maternal grandparents retired from the ministry and came to live with us. Our household joyfully exploded with fresh produce from Papa's award-winning gardens. Nanny's home cooking took center stage. Along with the Saturday chicken-neck-wringing exhibition, fruit and vegetable preserving, and home-made ice cream churning came grandparent games that were a delight for the soul until both Nanny and Papa died before our reign as teenagers began.

How any of us lived through the madness of those years, only God knows. Each child was so uniquely aggravating; Mama should have been awarded combat pay. Although I often wanted to send her a sympathy card, I was probably the most irritating one of all. I always needed to know if there was logic in her decision making—if her decisions were the best for all concerned. I was a frequent recipient of the "Mama look" during many a teachable moment when she taught her "Sistah Girl" a thing or two. Since she was teaching full-time now, her work and children at school became her oasis. When she was home, we three became her guinea pigs for every exciting idea or project she could muster up for her students.

Once Mama's children were off to college, she sold our lovely old barn of a house. I was happy to be absent for that event. Gone was our childhood place to dream, play, and pray. Mama continued to demonstrate courage and grace as she moved to a newer, smaller space and watched her adult children come and go as she worked and worked. By the time my brother and I had graduated from college, she had settled into a teaching position at a community college. Life was finally looking pretty rosy for Mama.

The ink was still wet on my college diploma from the University of Texas at Austin when I was hired as a college instructor in San Antonio. As God would have it, Mama and I ended up teaching at the same college. Her passion for imparting knowledge had already become legend; my tenure at the college was an adventure in a vocation I swore as a child I would never claim as my own. In spite of myself, I learned to love teaching at a college where my Mama was known as a fast-talking, fast-walking ball of inspiration who would roll with you, under you, around you, or, if necessary, over you to force you to love life and learning.

Seven months after starting my teaching career, I told Mama that I was marrying my best friend and longtime love, Clinton Davis. As my marriage grew in friendship and love, so did Mama's love and respect for my husband. A romantic, Clinton brought her flowers and gifts from the heart each time he gave me the same. He fast became her loving son and attentive companion as they planned activities together and checked on one another throughout the day. They especially enjoyed plotting against me during my more unattractive stubborn moments. Throughout twenty-eight years of marriage, Clinton and I shared our love and our lives with Browning Anna Louvenia McKinney Samples.

It has been three years since my husband's passing. Mama and I continue learning together about the beauty of pain, the demands of joy, and the preciousness of every moment. In *Things My Mama Told Me: The Wisdom That Shapes Our Lives,* I want to pay tribute to the mother who has taught me most everything I know...and to honor your story through my story.

Celebrate with me the gifts our mothers have given us. As you read the "Mamaisms" that open each story—powerful bits of wisdom from my mother's vast collection—look back on your own life to glean lessons perhaps forgotten. In these "Mama Moments," let us celebrate one another and the glory our Creator has instilled in each of us.

RULES

Your rules are your life tools.

—　—

I make the rules in this house,
and you will gladly follow them.

—　—

Whoever pays the bills rules.

CLASSROOM OF LIFE

I cannot believe how much my adult students hate my rules!" I complained to Mama. "Like not wearing a hat inside the classroom."

"It is a different age," Mama responded. "Students see nothing wrong with dressing the way they want to and saying and doing what they please. Of course, I wouldn't have any of that when I was teaching."

"Well, what did you do differently from what I am doing? You certainly had some of the same rules. And it has been years since your retirement, and students are still talking about your rules and classroom practices."

Mama was happy to hear the news about her legacy and to further elaborate on her command of her classroom. "I walked into the room like I owned the building. And I demanded respect. I told those students that if the president himself walked into my classroom, he would follow my rules and do what I told him to do. Long before academic freedom and long after I signed on the dotted line, I ran my classroom by the rules I established on the first day. And as far as you crumb snatchers are concerned, you followed my rules in this household just like my students. If you have no rules, you have little chance for a civilized gathering."

My words piggybacked on her message. "You don't have to remind me. I thought we were in military boot camp at times! 'Do this, do that, jump, walk, stay, sit, run, pray.' A lotta praying," I teased. "I used to pray to go to bed early so you wouldn't give me another thing to do."

She was quick with her one-upmanship line. "Did it work?"

"Well, I believe in prayer. I also believe that you were in cahoots with God. So, no…most of the time my prayers to be relieved from duty did not come to fruition. Are you happy?"

I let her have the last word so she wouldn't have to take it. "Thank goodness," she purred. "Our God does work in wondrous ways."

ENCOURAGEMENT

*Never let wrinkles set up housekeeping
in your soul.*

—

*When the music stops playing,
create a new tune.*

—

*Folks who really love you
understand things about you
that sometimes don't make
a doggone bit of sense.*

THE PITY PARTY

I could tell by the sound of her voice that she was not feeling well. That usually happened when she burned the candle at both ends. Nothing to do but go see about her. As I journeyed to her home, I remembered what I once heard someone say when asked how he felt about caring for his parents at this time in his life. His response was simple: "What an honor…what a sweet, sweet task." A most appropriate response in my case as well.

Once at Mama's house, I asked the usual questions: "What have you eaten?" "When did you last eat?" "Have you taken your medicine?" Responses came with hesitation. Was there anything I could do? "How about a boyfriend?" I said with my best poker face. She rolled her seventy-eight-year-old eyes in a fashion that didn't contain her usual mischief.

Then I figured it out. Why hadn't I realized it sooner? She simply had the blues. That was fixable! I whipped out my pocket piano harmonica and dark glasses. After she began laughing at my best Ray Charles imitation, a better idea jumped up and slapped me. She needed truth and cheer. After all, she was my mother, my friend.

"I have a new poem. I need your advice and criticism." Advice, criticism—I knew she was hooked when she changed her poor-me position to a I-shall-not-be-moved posture. She listened intently as I recited.

Never…never are you too old to dance. Never.

Your heart can still laugh—memories can still hold fast.
You never are too old to dance!

And never are you too old, too young, too anything-else to
    dance. Never!
Your mind is ever bright with imaginings and light.
Never should you be too *anything* to dance.

Never are you too tall or short, wide or miniscule, poor or
    rich, hopeless or hopeful.
Never too intelligent. Never too mentally challenged. Never
    too disabled to dance.

Dance your dreams. Dance your pain. Dance your uncertain-
    ness. Just dance!

Tell the world your one-of-a-kind-ness.
Give your sashay, your rhythm, step, kick, and sway—any
    talents you own—and dance!

Speak words. Shout volumes in your dance of life.
Dance memories. Capture moments, Child Bright! Take
    flight and dance…

Soar! Fly! Spread your wings!

For in you, Creativity. In you, Spontaneity. In you, a dance like no other.

Dance who you are now and for all time.

Goodness, that is you. Greatness, also you. Music is your soul.

Breathe your being.

You, spirit-wide this moment.

Dance joy and thankfulness. Dance visions of touch. Dance hands. Dance smiles.

This moment your sacred trust. Your only promise…this moment.

Dance your timeless soul-truths.

Stretch beyond yourself in celebration of God-gifts.

Dance with the knowledge of glorious acceptance.

Dance now…yes, now.

Dance, dance…

Just dance!

Tears rolled down Mama's beautiful dark face. Amazing…how absolutely wonderful it still feels to bring pleasure to a parent.

PARENTING

Your children are on loan to you
for an indefinite amount of time.

———

Parenting is not an exact science;
you do the best you can...
and pray a whole lot.

———

One day you will learn:
If you choose to be a good parent,
it will be the hardest work
that you will ever do.

A BEAUTIFUL THING

*H*ow in the world did she do it? How did she cook and clean and wash and iron and organize everyone while managing to speak softly, authoritatively, and lovingly? How did she work outside the home and still come home to do more work? How did she manage to go back to school to get her teaching degree and still help us and other children in the neighborhood with our studies and our extracurricular activities? What kind of stuff was she made of to go without food or sleep or money and still keep us clean, well fed, loved, and on course with our lives? There never seemed to be time for her to play or be alone to hear herself think. Everything and everyone seemed to come before her.

Was this a normal mothering thing? Was this what parents across the world did to keep their families together? Since Daddy died, she was the mother, the father, the cook, the housekeeper, the teacher, the breadwinner, the spiritual leader, the counselor, the so-much-more. What about *her* life? This question was ablaze in my adolescent thoughts.

"Mom, when will you take time to do something for yourself?" I asked her one day.

"When there are no more things to do for all of you," she replied matter-of-factly.

"But that will be a long time from now. You need to start having some fun. Go out with some of your friends. Buy yourself a new dress."

She smiled. "I appreciate your concern. One day there will be time for that. I choose to be a full-time parent…it is a beautiful thing." She kept on folding the clothes in the baskets, sorting them in piles. As I joined her, she began singing one of her favorite songs, "O Master, Let Me Walk with Thee." I hummed along.

After prayers that night, I couldn't sleep. Mama seemed to be sacrificing so much to be a single parent. How could it really be "beautiful" with all the daily headaches? Yet for the most part she seemed to be happy.

It was only in retrospect that I came to understand her innermost feelings about parenting. Despite all of Mama's "doing" for us, she always managed to commit to "being" with us. She gave us her heart, her mind, and her soul. She traveled with us emotionally. She listened and laughed and questioned and challenged and insisted on excellence. And it was the being with us that was so very important to us. It was the being that brought her so much joy.

In my profession, God sends me more than one hundred adult students every semester. In my heart, they are my children. Not a day goes by without my thinking about Mama's being present with us when we were in her daily care. Because of her powerful example, it comes naturally to me to bring that same gift to family, friends, and students alike.

GENEROSITY

*Generous hearts are created
from everyday acts of kindness.*

— • —

*Be generous to someone
—friend, foe, or stranger—
at least once a day.*

— • —

Make generosity a lifetime habit.

THE RIGHT THING TO DO

*M*ama often talked to us about her "other children"—the young people in her class who were our adopted brothers and sisters. If one of her classroom children needed clothing or supplies, she found a way to get what was needed and still keep us afloat with necessities. It was amazing how she would juggle everyone's needs but her own.

Later, these teaching-learning sessions prompted questions from me. Where was this money to help others coming from? Meals were ordinary and economical. And Mama sewed most of our clothes and played Mrs. Fix-it around the house. There was never any extra money, so it wasn't being deducted from the food or household budget. We barely scraped by on her teacher's salary. I was simply puzzled. Why all the sacrifice, especially where she was personally concerned?

"Because it is the right thing to do," she solemnly replied when I pressed her. I mused aloud that she was too busy, that maybe she should try to do a little less of the right thing for others and more of the right thing for herself.

She came back with a you-had-better-believe-this smile. "As bad as you think we might be doing, we are in great shape compared to others. If I have something to share, I share it in appreciation for the life we have been so fortunate to have and to know." I knew she hadn't finished talking, so I just sat there and waited for the next installment. "It comes back to doing the right thing. When you do the right thing for others, it is simply what you are supposed to do. And it is a feeling like no other." I stayed still. I could almost feel the temperature rising as Mama spoke with passion. "And do you know what is one of the marvelous results of doing the right thing? Simply this: You like what you see in the mirror when you wake up in the morning. You have to like what you see in the mirror!"

That was a tall order. Doing the right thing because it was the right thing…and liking yourself for making whatever sacrifice you had to make to ensure that would happen. Was that why Mama gathered the best roses from her garden, arranged them in vases, and took them to the sick and shut-ins? As our garden overflowed with vegetables, was that why she hurried to make sure they would go to others before they spoiled? When she couldn't make timely telephone calls to people who had lost family members, was that why she took such time to find the right card with the best words? When her students came to school with urgent needs, was that why she took it upon herself to solve their problems? So many everyday little-big things she did for us and others—all simply because it was the right thing to do.

It took a long time for that lesson to register in my mind and heart. When it finally made sense to me, I discovered a different perspective about self-sacrifice in particular and life in general. Now when I make the time to buy flowers from the wholesale market and design flower arrangements for those in need, I always think of Mama and her generous ways. My bouquets are not as beautiful as hers; still, I know that if I just keep trying every day to be big-hearted like Mama, in time the flowers I give away will take on a beauty all their own.

COMMUNICATION

*Don't let your mouth write a check
your body can't cash.*

—•—

Don't let your tongue overload your teeth.

—•—

*You don't have to holler
for me to hear you.*

STRAIGHTEN UP
AND FLY RIGHT

*M*ama's most effective form of communication hardly ever included the king's English. It was bold or subtle—hardly ever in between.

There was the powerful look that could whip you into shape. If you were close by and acting up at home or in public, she often said nothing. She just looked at you in a way that made you know you had better straighten up and fly right. The look only had to be seen once by the actor-upper.

Distinctly powerful in its own right was "the eye." The eye would catch you across the room, playground, or park and bring you to a screeching halt. No words were necessary—just the eye.

In rare cases, the spanking would come next. Private or public, the spanking had your name on it if you pushed your luck too far. When I saw that whipping coming, I would quickly apologize again and again. But it was too late, and Mama wouldn't back down from her promise. "Anytime you are grown enough to let your mouth write a check your little body can't cash, you are ripe for a whipping. And you earned it because you ignored all the other chances to make things right." Then the dramatic pause. "Sistah Girl, you need to realize that the world won't give you that many chances." Then she would add salt to the wound with the infamous statement, "I'm only whipping you because I love you."

As if the spanking wasn't humiliating enough, she had two special types of whipping materials. There was her hand. The hand didn't last long because we soon saw it coming and ran away from its path. Later came the switch. The switch was much more painful because we had to go and get it from one of our trees in the yard. If we came back with a less than sturdy whipping implement, Mama sent us back as many times as necessary to find just the right piece of disciplinary equipment. Believe me when I say that we tried to pick the right switch the first time.

Mama employed one of two predictable communication styles when administering a spanking. The no-talking style of spanking was over in a flash. The talking style of spanking lasted longer and came in the form of the syllable beating—one that had an introduction, body, and conclusion to it. In the introduction, you were made to listen to a sermonette—the purpose of the punishment. In the body of the beating, you were actually spanked and talked to in syllables, like "I told you not to go in-to the cem-e-ter-y to ride your bike." The body of the punishment went on to explain—in syllables—what could have happened and why it shouldn't happen again. The conclusion was succinct. Mama would say, "I hope you've learned your lesson. Now go to your room until I tell you to come out sometime later this year."

My sister and brother and I were never hurt or scarred. Never were we ignorant about the reason for our punishment. The few spankings we got simply served as wake-up calls for us when our mother's other forms of communication failed to get through.

As we grew up and Mama retired from spanking us, everyone became more verbal. One day I was in my room at the front of our house, and Mama was in the kitchen in the back of the house when I decided I needed critical advice about an outfit and was too lazy to go and converse with her. I was hollering at the top of my lungs. She didn't answer. I kept hollering. Still she didn't answer. Finally, in frustration I went to her.

"Mama, why didn't you answer me?" I demanded.

Her look declared that I had better watch my tone of voice. "I think you sometimes forget that you are my child and I am your parent. You need to have civilized, face-to-face communication if you have something important you must talk about. I won't respond when you choose to holler instead of speak respectfully."

By the time Mama had finished expounding on the value of her brand of communication, my previously pressing problem was lost to me. I had forgotten what I'd wanted to say.

PRIDE

You can be two-bit smart
if you want to...
it will catch up with you.

—　—

Don't let your pride
put you in an early grave.

—　—

You might think you're the cat's meow,
but I'll guarantee you
there are plenty of folks
who think the sun rises and sets on them, too.

A SCHEME GONE BAD

*I*n elementary school, I loved being a tomboy in our neighborhood where the boys thought they were the alpha and the omega. Girls were outnumbered thirty to three, and I was the only female interested in dealing with the guys on their terms.

What did I like about these guys? They were protective and fun loving. They let me play games with them, especially baseball. They made me rough and tough and ready for any nonsense that might come my way in a world where gender was sometimes disrespected. They taught me how to understand male thinking and actions. It wasn't easy, but I held my own most of the time. I learned how to assert my authority as an equal whenever and however I could.

On one particular Sunday, I had a rare opportunity to make a few rules of my own…if only I could get to the baseball field first. The boys needed some equipment that I possessed. My chances for being captain of the team that day were high if I could just get there ahead of everyone else. Instead of being picked last for a position because I was a girl, I could be a captain, make the team selections, and say how the cow ate the cabbage. Before any of that could happen, however, I had to attend the morning church services.

Before leaving for church, I put my plan in motion. I figured that I could save time getting out to the playground after church by putting on my play clothes under my Sunday dress. All I really needed to do was roll up my pant legs above my knees. Between the petticoats and the wide skirt, there was plenty of room to hide the long tail of my casual shirt and jeans. Who would notice?

At church the service went smoothly. In fact, for some reason the sermon was unusually brief, and everyone was unknowingly on schedule with my plan. Next was communion. I bowed at the altar to receive my wafers and grape juice and then rose to make my way to the aisle leading back to the pew where I was sitting. Since the line of people snaking back to their seats was long and slow, I had time to daydream about the baseball game soon to come. I was going to be the best team captain those boys had ever seen. I would demonstrate what it really meant to be a leader.

While I slowly made my way back to my seat, a sickening feeling found its way to my stomach as one of Mama's many sermonettes popped into my mind. "Pride goeth before a fall," I could hear her say as one of my pant legs started coming down while I was trapped in a holding pattern with all the communion goers. I put my legs closer together and immediately developed a slower gait. Realizing I had not applied enough pressure to stop the unfolding, I tightened my squeeze and sank lower to the floor as I steadily worked my way down the aisle. I must have looked as though I needed to go to the rest room, because an usher rushed to my aid. The more I courteously declined assistance, the more she tried to help me, and the faster the pant leg came down. As if that wasn't bad enough, the other pant leg began unraveling. At this point I knew I was in deep trouble as I viewed the look of disappointment in the good sisters' and brothers' faces on those aisle seats.

Where was Mama? I looked around and was relieved that I couldn't locate her watchful eye. So I made a run for it once the aisle was clear. And run I did—as fast as I could from the center aisle, out the vestibule doors, to the outer doors and parking lot. My mission was to get to the rest room on the other side of the church without Mama knowing about my dastardly deed. My hope was that maybe she hadn't noticed this spectacle in the Lord's house. Possible but not probable. I could only hope she was half as embarrassed as I was.

A conversation about this little scheme-gone-bad of mine was never initiated. Mama never officially let me know what she knew. She said nothing. She only seemed to sing more songs around the house than usual that Sunday. Secular and religious songs that made you think more about your life and where it was going. Songs like "Nobody Knows the Trouble I've Seen," "We'll Understand It Better By and By," "Precious Lord, Take My Hand," and "Were You There?" Her melodic messages convinced me that she knew more than she was telling.

I never made it to the playground that day—first or last. Mama insisted that I looked tired and needed to stay inside and rest. I certainly didn't object for fear that she would offer worse alternatives. Not once during the rest of the day did Mama inquire about my well-being or bring up the church incident. I was grateful she was giving me her cold treatment and nothing more. Mama was not a Christian when it came to her children being disrespectful in God's house.

In the days to come, I quietly moved about the house in as many opposite directions of Mama's path as I could conjure up. I felt as if I had been spared this time. My pride almost put me in what I thought might be an early grave.

THOUGHTFULNESS

There is no law requiring people
to be kind; be kind anyway.

—

Courtesy is more than a "please"
or "thank you."
It is respect in action.

—

Everyday courtesy to everybody
is a mark of good character.

NOTES OF BLESSING

*T*hank-you notes again?!" I complained. "We write thank-you notes for everything, *and* we write 'thinking of you' notes for everyone! We are writing all the time. Why not just call and thank them? Why not just stop by on the way to church and say hello or thank you?"

Mama carefully considered my words. "Hmmm…you just might have a good idea. Let's plan a visit or phone call—*along with* the notes you will send," she quipped.

My plan was failing. I wanted less work, less writing. I needed to find a better angle quickly. "Mama, I meant that maybe we could visit or call *instead of* sending a note."

My mother pretended to ignore me; she did that when she wanted me to hear myself. I had probably overstepped my bounds. *Think quickly, Sistah Girl. Think of something to fix this situation.*

Before I could deliver my next verbal ploy, her words came simultaneously with a hand on hip. With braced posture came new height. Sermon was forthcoming.

"Have you forgotten how many folks have *no one* to remember them? Do you realize how *one* thoughtful act can change a life forever? Do you know how few people get *good news* in the mail?" As she came closer, I wasn't sure if I should run or sit and suffer. She took a breath and continued. "Your handwritten note is something more than community service, Sistah Girl. It is an example of your home training. Who you are is also a reflection of who I am and how you honor your family name, including those family members who are no longer with us."

More silence before the finale. "This little bit of sunshine you share in a handwritten note can help someone, somewhere, make it through the day…or week…or month…or even the year."

She turned and reached into the cupboard. Out came a box which she placed on the kitchen table. "Maybe if you read a little about how simple acts of kindness can positively impact the lives of others, you will better understand."

I sat still for a long while, reading thank-you notes people had sent to Mama…notes thanking her for her gestures of appreciation and for raising thoughtful children who expressed the same. These were sobering moments. Over the years the recipients of our thinking-of-you and thank-you notes had been so grateful. A brief look into their hearts quickly showed me that small efforts from me and my family members had produced great joy.

Suddenly my complaining spirit was replaced with humble gratitude. I was glad Mama had set the bar higher than my little eyes could see. The power of kindness, especially thoughtfully presented through the written word, is a loving courtesy I have practiced ever since.

HOSPITALITY

There is always room for one more.

—◦—

Sit like you got a family.

—◦—

There is no "this is mine" here.
This is ours.

PINTO BEANS

I do not know how she did it. She could feed everyone who walked through the door. Nothing fancy. Usually beans—1 of 365 ways. Most often pinto beans. So there were pinto beans and rice. Pinto beans and cornbread. Chili with pinto beans. Pinto beans à la carte. Pinto beans and chicken. Pinto beans and potatoes. Pinto beans and ground-beef casserole. Maybe even a pinto bean fondue or soufflé I elected not to remember. You name it and she would come up with it. Each dish designed to provide for the masses—should they appear.

"Why beans all the time, Mama?" was my query.

"Beans are good for your heart. Beans help you fill up when your appetite is great. Beans help your digestion." I giggled, and she smiled at me as she continued. "Besides, if you cook with love and serve the meal accordingly, it doesn't matter what people are eating. What matters is that they feel welcomed with open arms."

I sat quietly for a while and watched my mother prepare for the meal. She took extra time to make the food look attractive. As she laid out the place mats and silverware, thought and time were given to table decorations that might add to the meal's celebration. In her simple, hands-on way, Mama was saying, "You are being cared for."

I felt the need to say something. "You have such a big heart, Mama. You make everyone feel welcome. One of my teachers was talking about you when she used the word *hospitable*. You are hospitable. Many people have trouble being hospitable, but you do it naturally."

When you are young, you don't always want to be like a parent; you just want to be youthful and different. But at times you see something in a parent that you long to emulate. When it came to having a spirit of hospitality, I knew at age eleven that I wanted to grow up to be just like my mother.

TRUTH

Everything that is done in the dark
will eventually come to light.

— —

Every shut eye ain't asleep;
every good-bye ain't gone.

— —

God sees everything.

BUTTERBALL TO THE RESCUE

*I*t was navy bean day. Navy beans and a little meat and some salad. For my money that meant it was Butterball's opportunity to do his best work. Butterball was our family dog and a non-pedigree resident friend.

Now the rule in the house was to keep Butterball outside. But my brother, the only boy and the baby in the family, had a way of convincing Mama to do many things he wanted her to do. Enter Butterball. He was in the house that day as a result of my little brother's charming influence.

Fact: I hated navy beans. They looked bland and tasted bland. They were ugly and awful to force down my throat. I would have to be starving before I would willingly eat navy beans. No matter how many times I conveyed my dislike of those beans to Mama, she never understood. Beans were Mama's mainstay, and navy beans were her nourishment of choice this day.

Butterball was under the table waiting for his crumbs when I offered him the first group of navy beans. So far so good. Each time Mama left the room, a few more navy beans left my plate. This was a slow process, but the mission was being accomplished. Good ol' Butterball—willing and able.

The last of the navy beans were being ushered down Butterball's throat when he felt compelled to regurgitate all the beans onto the floor. I hurriedly volunteered to clean up the mess before Mama could see what was happening. Not fast enough. Not only did she see the evidence, but she also suspected the Butterball food relief program had been under way for some time. What was there to say? *Say nothing,* I told myself sternly.

After the cleanup, I asked to be excused from the table and be allowed to go to bed early. "Not so fast, Missy," Mama answered sweetly. "There is something you need to do." I wondered what in the world I had to do now. I had finished my homework and cleaned up the mess. She didn't seem angry as she got up from the table and headed toward the kitchen...or at least I hoped she wasn't angry. I really needed to get to bed before she had time to think about it anymore.

Reenter Mama with a bowl of navy beans. "You didn't finish your dinner, Missy. Eat up!"

"But I'm not hungry!" I cried.

"Well, you'd better get hungry," she shot back. "You can eat those beans or lose your privileges for two weeks. It's up to you."

The tone in her voice assured me that eating the navy beans was a far cry better than pushing the issue. Spoonful by spoonful, I worked my way through the torture of eating those cold, hard, and hideous beans. It took me an hour...but I ate them. And while I was eating them, my brother teased me as Butterball watched. I eventually had to pretend they were sweet white jelly beans in disguise before each one successfully traveled to my mouth and down my throat.

When I finally made my way to the bedroom, Mama found me there. "Had you told me the truth, we could have possibly come to terms. I could have given you more salad and a few beans—or no beans! In this case," she explained, "your dishonesty cost you. There will always be a price to pay for dishonesty." I was momentarily flabbergasted by my own foolishness. To think that all I'd needed to do was tell the truth...to go to her respectfully, explain my feelings, and ask for more salad and little or no navy beans! Both Butterball and I could have been spared our upset stomachs.

Years later when I brought up the topic again, Mama began laughing about the incident. She then acknowledged that even if I had told the truth about my dislike for those beans, she would not have necessarily excused me from eating them. *Face it, Sistah Girl,* I told myself. *Mama always wins.*

EVIL

Watch out! Evil is a sneaky darn thing.

— —

Evil is bodacious and fearless;
if you see it coming, fight it with faith.

— —

You can't always stop evil…
but you do have a choice
as to whether or not you support it
through what you say and do.

CHOICES

*H*e lied on me," I screamed as I ran into the house. "I didn't do it. I was framed!"

My anger had hit an apex. "And he told me that he knew I didn't do it but that he was going to lie on me anyway." My cries sounded ugly and torturous—even to me. How could my friend do this to me?

As she continued her kitchen ritual, Mama just looked at me. "What happened?"

"I was betrayed and lied on—that's what happened! All I did was say I *only* wanted to be friends—not girlfriend and boyfriend. He got angry and promised to make my life miserable. And then he started spreading lies on me. Telling everyone in our school any untrue things about me he could invent!"

"And if these things were untrue, why are you upset?" she responded.

"Because I was trying to be nice when no one else wanted to be bothered with him. He's a jerk. And his lies hurt!"

The floodgates were now officially open. I cried and cried, my head cradled in my arms on the kitchen table. I was relieved by Mama's silence. I didn't want to be preached to, on top of being lied on.

At last, though, a message worth listening to. "Throughout your life, people are going to do evil things," Mama began. "Snakes come in every age, color, culture, ethnicity, religion, and creed. Learn from them or get bit by them."

She handed me a roll of toilet tissue. I stopped crying just long enough to wonder, *Isn't my pain worthy of facial tissue?*

"Go ahead—have yourself a good cry. If I were in your shoes, I would be upset too. Few things hurt more than the betrayal of a so-called friend." Mama let me blow my nose before she continued. "Evil acts catch you off guard. Often they appear to come from people who are bold and fearless. In truth, most of these people are really afraid, hurt, or cowardly. You cannot let them win by going to battle with them and their evil. The minute they know they have been effective in baiting or hurting you, they win."

My tears were beginning to subside as I looked up to notice her stirring with a vengeance the hash in her cast-iron skillet—as if a similar hurtful memory had found its way back to her mind. Turning off the fire, Mama waved her cooking spoon like a weapon. "I'll say it again because it bears repeating. Learn from them, or just get bit by them. It's your choice whether or not you let their poison infect you."

My choice…mine alone. Mama explained evil in a way I could never forget. Somehow I couldn't begin to imagine ever seeing a snake again—slithering or on two legs—in quite the same way.

COMPASSION

Have a kind word for friends and family every day.

———

Life is not always about you.

———

Sometimes you need to let your heart tell you what to do.

A NEW SONG

*M*y mother was crying. She was trying to hide her tears. Her hand darted from apron pocket to that mahogany skin, the handkerchief aimed to catch each falling drop before discovery. Even with Daddy dying and all the hard times that went with his passing, I had never seen my mother cry. My nine-year-old person moved to comfort her. She seemed surprised that she had not disguised her pain well enough to move through it before anyone noticed.

"Nothing," she replied when I asked her what was wrong. My concern grew. Nothing always meant something. And she kept crying. Now it was a shaking crying and a strange low moaning of hurt in a place faraway—yet ever so close.

"May I do something for you, Mama?"

"Nothing," was again her response. Since this was coming from a woman who had always said that everyone can at least do *something*, I was at a loss. My mind went back to the times she had comforted me. Sometimes it was a soft pat on the back or a word of compassion and love. Often it was a look from those deep brown eyes that confirmed the message, "Everything will be all right."

I moved closer to her and patted her on the back and repeated several times, "It will be all right." I found myself saying those words over and over until Mama's shaking stopped. But she was still crying. The tissues and handkerchief were soaked with despair as she lifted the apron to her face.

Desperate to find the right words, I remembered an old church song. She loved the song. Maybe my off-key, improvised version would help. Hopefully it wouldn't kill her.

"Jesus loves me! This I know, for the Bible tells me so. Little ones to Him belong; they are weak, but He is strong." As I got to, "Yes, Jesus loves me!" she lifted her head and began singing with me.

I will never forget that moment when the compassion Mama had taught me came back to her through me...and she sang again.

PRAYER

You need to spend more time on your knees
so you can have a better time on your feet.

———

Prayer is an everyday, every-night,
and in-between conversation with God.

———

Faith is seeing light where darkness prevails.

IN TIMES OF WHY?

*I*t was elementary school. It was third grade. And it was my classmate and friend who was reported dead on the morning news.

I wouldn't talk about it. The principal and teachers at school didn't talk about it—except to announce he was dead. Everyone seemed to hope that the news of his death would just go away. It didn't. Neither did the deep sense of loss.

The newspaper said he was playing with a gun when it accidentally discharged. Questions flooded my mind. *Why would he do that? Didn't he know that guns were dangerous? Was he in pain those final moments? Did he suffer? Was he alone when he took his last breath? Did he know we loved him?*

And I wondered why God let this happen to him.

When Mama told us the news, she searched for the right words. "Sometimes the good die young," she said. "He's with God now. Let's pray for his family."

I prayed. Then I prayed some more. The questions and sadness didn't go away. The day before he left us, he had played baseball in the street with the neighborhood kids. And earlier that same day he had acted like a class clown. His sweet, broad-faced grin and cocky swagger was the last picture we saw of him as he waved good-bye and shouted, "Tomorrow...see you tomorrow." Why did he leave us? Why in such a sudden and brutal way?

Without telling Mama, a few days later I went alone to see his parents. They were not home. But there was a wreath on the door with his picture. He had the same sweet, cocky smile on his face that he wore the day before his death. It was a comfort to sit on his porch and pray for him and his family.

As I walked home, I recalled one of Mama's favorite sayings: "When you sing, you pray twice." From the heart of my being jumped a song of tribute to my friend with the hope that if I sang really loud, it would be like praying twice. I sang until I could sing no more. Loud. I sang loud.

And over time I have convinced myself that my song on that day was a tune my sweet friend heard in heaven.

AUTHORITY

I brought you into this world...
I can take you out.

———

What makes you think this is a request?

———

I have forgotten more tricks
than you will ever know or remember.

THERE COMES A TIME

There comes a time when you think you know more than your parents. After all, they simply cannot really understand your position. They were never young with similar problems. Such a time had come in our household. I was the ripe old age of thirteen.

My desire to go out and play in the all-star street tournament was greater than my commitment to my studies. I argued the point that my teacher did not assign homework for that day. My mother replied, "You always have homework in real life. There is always something you can do to be better if you strive for excellence. So, Missy, you can create suitable homework, or I will be happy to create some for you."

Only a half-wit would want my mother to take on that task. I "yes ma'am-ed" my way out of the room and went in search of flash cards. Aha! I spied a box of spelling cards that held all the words I'd previously learned. After making enough productive noise, I took the box to Mama and requested her help in a review. Hands full, she stopped what she was doing and sat down at the kitchen table to test me on the cards.

The high drama began. I hesitated as I painstakingly tried to spell each word. I would fool her with my suffering act—certain evidence that I was making a true effort. Fifteen words later she still was not satisfied. My confidence grew…in a two-bit-slick kind of way. I increased the tempo of my presentation. Fifty cards later I was spelling-bee perfect. I could smell victory as the neighborhood make-shift playground grew closer by the second.

Silence invaded my playtime daydream. A few minutes had lapsed before I came back to the world. I caught Mama surveying me carefully. What was she thinking? How long had she been watching me? Finally she spoke. "Let's tackle the next fifty."

I was hurt and angry that my plan had not worked. "I did everything you said I needed to do. Why can't you just let me go play? It is getting dark. The team needs me."

My cry landed on deaf ears. Bold sister that I thought I was, I decided to elevate the volume of my voice with a bit of theatrical foot stamping. "But why…*why, why?* Why can't you let me just go…just this one time? *Why?*"

Browning Louvenia's posture and attitude changed before my eyes. Her foot began tapping as she cocked her head to the side. Then the deep breaths. I realized I had gone too far.

Hand on hip, she bored holes into me with her eyes before announcing with finality, "Why? Why indeed! *Because I said so!*"

I knew that if I truly valued life, I was not to say another word. And my little inside voice told me that if I wasn't careful, I would be doomed to spend the rest of my childhood indoors.

HOME

Home is wherever you find—and give—love.

— —

In this house, everyone
should be made to feel at home.

— —

You are safe here…you are at home.

THE PALMETTO PALACE

*W*e lived in an ancient barn of a house on North Palmetto Street. With its high ceilings, many four-by-six windows, and wooden floors, it was a palace in its own right. It was also the neighborhood gathering place and a home away from home for many other folks besides us. For each member of the human family who abided in or entered our home, Mama's directive was clear: "This house is home to every one of God's children. All are welcome, and no one goes unnoticed."

This house had enormous rooms and unmistakable character. There were few doors to separate us and one floor furnace to gather round. The kitchen table—which doubled for dining—was in the center of the house. Strangely enough, the kitchen was one of the busiest, yet smallest rooms; you had to be small enough to get in there and squeeze through or make do. When Daddy was alive, his bigness allowed no one to share the space—except Mama.

For me the most outstanding spaces in our house were the porches. Wide porches hugging the house. And on both porches were lounging places with Mama's special touch of fabric and greenery. The sun porch, in particular, fanned freedom with furniture that loved each body and exotic plants that beckoned you to stretch, to reach beyond yourself. Your heartstrings could be tickled by the whispered invitation to dream. Mama's hope and faith were abundantly present in that room.

The Palmetto Palace was a house of innovation and creation. It was a home of acceptance and love. It was the center of the neighborhood. It was a resting place—a safe place—before you went off to the next thing. If ever there was a tangibly loved structure, it was this place that Mama made home.

It wasn't until one of my playmates sat beside me on our front porch one scorching Texas August day that I fully understood the beauty of our home. From his devilish nature came the most angelic words: "Coming to this house is like going to church."

It was a message that rang out like a steeple bell.

GRATITUDE

*Gratitude is an attitude that colors everything
you do and say.*

———

*When you learn to be grateful for everything
—the least and the most—
you shall embrace a spirit
of perpetual thanksgiving.*

———

Nothing is sadder than an ungrateful heart.

NEIGHBORHOOD MAMAS

Goodness knows I loved them. They were all storytellers, cooks, housekeepers, teachers, mediators, disciplinarians, church-goers, jills-of-all-trades, and a host of other titles I cannot begin to explain. They got things done and took care of the business of taking care of the children in the neighborhood—whether we liked it or not. They even had permission to spank Mama's children if all else failed.

All was well with me and my surrogate mamas until the week I stayed out on the corner a little too late with my playmates. My lateness was innocent enough; the problem was all those boys and one girl—me—acting rough and tough.

When I was reported to my mama by the neighborhood mamas, my mama had a long talk with me about decorum. "But, Mom, for miles around I am the only girl in a neighborhood of boys. I am not trying to misbehave. I just want to play baseball, build go-carts, and run track with them. None of them hurts me or flirts with me. They know better than to mess with me."

"I don't doubt what you're saying is true," Mama said. "Just don't let sundown catch you outside playing. I want you in the house when darkness comes round."

Could I leave the conversation at that? Oh, no. My big mouth went on to explain how I resented those mamas trying to ruin my life of play. I added that they were just busybodies who needed someone to talk about, someone to tell on.

Mama stopped me after the second line of my spouting off. "Hold it right there, Missy. You need to be glad that folks care about you enough to look out for your best interests. You should be thanking them for caring about you." She took a quick, deep breath. "If you want to preserve your leisure time, you had better appreciate their presence, smile, click your heels, and act as if you like their genuine concern for your well-being." Stopping for another breath, she added, "You can't begin to realize how fortunate you are. As safe as our neighborhood is, evil lurks. You could be a victim at any time. They love you like their own and want you to be safe."

Then the rascal in me had to mumble, "Well, I wish they would find someone else to love. They need to look in a different direction." I knew in an instant that I had gone too far. This last line got on Mama's last nerve. As she turned with the swiftness of a cougar and slammed her skillet down on the table, I became as small in stature as humanly possible. A rarely seen anger was on its way to full display.

"You want a different direction? I'll give you one. Your direction is to stay in the house after your homework is done and entertain yourself indoors for the next week!" With a deflating sigh of sadness she added the final nail to my coffin. "Nothing is sadder than an ungrateful heart. Nothing."

Punishment gives you time to think. And it hurts more than a spanking. Yet Mama's disappointment in me was the worst imaginable punishment of all.

Weeks later the topic of gratitude was revisited as we worked together on the sun porch. "You must always remember that no one makes it on his or her own. No one. There are many folks who help you. The least you can do—the very least—is to thank them."

And I do. Now, I do.

CREATIVITY

When you want something bad enough,
you will find a way to create it for yourself.

—

Creativity begins
with the visions in one's heart...
all else will follow.

—

True art is developing something beautiful
from the nothings of life.

WINDOW-SHOPPING

*M*ama had decided to take my siblings and me on a window-shopping tour. That meant every other child who could get permission to come with us would be stuffed in her car and off we would go.

Window-shopping with Mama was an adventure. Oohing and aahing and groaning, we would look and look in those department-store windows at things that were beautiful and things that were not. We would discuss what we saw and whether or not we would want it in our lives. It was free entertainment...and at times it was hard work. You see, Mama believed you should make your own toys or create your own books. That meant detailed planning, designing a prototype, refining the work, and figuring out a way to acquire materials and complete the final masterpiece. "You can do this," she would say. "God gave you a brain, a body, and a heart. You can make this yourself if you want to...if you really, really want it."

As I prepared for bed that evening, my head was full of images and ideas from the afternoon's adventure. We came home empty handed but renewed. No gifts had been purchased, no money exchanged. But the memories of those dolls and books and miscellaneous toys were still performing in my wide-awake imagination.

I knew there was no money for those things; still, I begged the question.

"Mama," I asked, "if we had all the money in the world, would you buy me those things we saw today?"

"Probably not, Sistah Girl," she replied.

I was shocked. Why wouldn't she buy me what I wanted and needed if she had all the money in the world? This was hard to understand. "Why not?" I prodded.

"Probably because you could make many—if not all—of those things yourself. In fact, you could make a much better toy or book or most anything else that we saw today. Your imagination could go hog-wild as you thought about it and planned for it and perfected it."

As she paused to collect her thoughts, her eyes sparkled like stars. "You see, Sistah Girl, something amazing happens when you try to create things for yourself. When we were children, we used our imagination and had the best fun you could ever begin to fathom. I remember having sock, stocking, and corncob dolls and sewing my books together before I wrote the stories and drew the pictures. And we made potato stamps—cutout designs on those Irish potatoes— and used them to decorate our wrappings and artwork!" Her excitement grew. "We used sticks for bats to play ball and managed to invent balls from the pieces of fabric and string we would gather. We played hide-and-seek with Papa and helped Nanny in the kitchen and with the gardening. You don't need a lot of things to have fun or create good times. In fact, I could even show you a few creative things to do with a cast-iron skillet!"

And that is how Mama gave us our beginning lessons in creativity...how she taught us to create something from nothing. We studied what others did—every aspect—and then tried to make our own versions of their creations as best we could.

Now, I must tell you, our dolls and books and paintings and go-carts made from "found" things didn't look as good or perform as well as some of the store-bought ones. But it sure felt good to know that we had done our best...and that we had made a decent showing. In fact, we always had a one-of-a-kind creation.

CONFIDENCE

If you want people to believe in you,
start by believing in yourself.

——

You can if you think you can.

——

Confidence comes each time
you give your best,
learn from it,
and then try to do better.

RENAISSANCE MAMA

*M*y confidence waned as I heard daily at school how brilliant my sister and brother were in all their courses. The praises were continuous. I knew I wasn't the brightest light on the humanity tree, but that was no excuse for teachers and principals to constantly remind me I wasn't an academic genius like my siblings. As if that wasn't bad enough, I shot myself in the foot with my own negative talk about possibly not trying hard enough. In the end, however, I just could not accept myself as the failure my academic elders thought me to be. How grateful I was to God that this nonacceptance was in tandem with Mama's thinking. The last thing I needed to do was to give up on myself. But how could I build my confidence in an environment of academic doubt?

When I spoke with Mama about this, she said matter-of-factly, "It is hard for folks to believe in you when you do not believe in yourself. Each day I see you walk and talk with less confidence. So we are going to begin a self-improvement program to build your self-assurance."

First she suggested I start working on my posture. "When you walk into a room, people see you and form an immediate opinion.

Walk in with pride. Hold your head high." Then she gave me a book to put on top of my head. Every day I had to practice walking with pride—with that book perfectly balanced on my noggin.

The next thing she did was to build my confidence in book knowledge. I made better than average grades but hardly ever straight A's. When she took all of us to the library weekly, she made sure that I found and checked out the biographies of great men and women. The idea was to help me identify with real stories of successful people and be reassured that greatness comes from a personal passion. She assured me that all of us have such vivacity hidden within, like gold. Each individual has to mine that gold, refine it, and develop a positive plan of action for using it. "Surround yourself with the best people in books—living or dead. Then find like persons in real life. Remember, great people come from every background and circumstance imaginable. Seek out the ones with admirable character and honorable behavior."

Mama then introduced us to the museums and arts organizations. "Keep art around you. Women and men are more civilized when the arts find a home in their hearts. Hear different types of music. See different plays, musicals, and dance recitals. Take visual art classes whenever possible. And dance. Never forget to dance."

In time there was also exposure to scouting, tennis, and piano lessons. We were blessed with a Renaissance Mama—eager to help us feel confident in our small world and a larger universe of people, places, and things.

There were days in my childhood when I wished I could just go to the corner drugstore and buy pounds of self-assurance to go, to use as needed. Mama's children didn't have much time for that kind of fantasy, however. We were too busy working at the everyday behaviors that eventually result in a deep, abiding confidence.

EDUCATION

You can have all the book sense
in the world,
but it won't help you much
if you don't have common sense
to go with it.

———

There are many ways to get an education;
schooling is only one.

———

Nothing is worse than an educated fool.

THE SHOULDERS ON
WHICH YOU STAND

*L*ike a wildfire, word of the paddling at school traveled fast. I thought I could make it home before all the neighbors volunteered their reports about what had happened in class that day.

I was wrong.

Halfway down the block, I could see my mother positioned by our gate. One part of me wanted to run the opposite direction; the other part knew better. So I kept walking and praying and walking and trying to prepare a story worthy of her attention and sympathetic to her ear. By the time I got to the gate, she had moved to the porch. And before I could open my mouth, Mama was standing at the front door waiting for me with a clear directive: "It is best that you don't say a thing just yet. Go take off your school clothes and meet me in the kitchen."

I stalled for time to create a credible story. I also knew a few extra minutes might help my mother calm down. After all, it was just a paddling. Everyone in the class had their bottoms spanked. It seemed to me that our brand-spanking-new sixth-grade teacher was only trying to assert his authority. And he was "fresh meat" to this veteran class of twelve-year-olds. It really wasn't our fault he couldn't control us…right?

The walk from the bedroom to the kitchen was longer than I ever remembered it to be. As I rounded the corner, Mama was sitting at the table looking into the distance. I noticed that my usual after-school snack was missing and the table was clear of everything but the Bible. This was serious.

"Mother," I quickly uttered in an effort to begin my defense. She motioned for me to be quiet and sit. And sit I did for what seemed like forever. It was a waiting game. She hoped I would think about my sin; she wanted me to clear the space in my little mind for a lifetime lesson. The silent treatment was always effective in cases like these. You wished she would just beat your behind and be done with it. Oh no, she wanted you to suffer. And I did.

Finally the words came. Slow and deliberate words. Simple and powerful words. The direction of the sermon was clear: "Do you realize that people died so you could have the right to go to school and get an education? Do you not understand that it is a privilege to be able to spend time in a safe environment to learn? Look here, Sistah Girl, to me this school business is something more than an investment of taxpayers' dollars. When I was your age…" Then she went on and on about how she and her sisters and brothers had to walk miles to school, about those cold biscuits and molasses in their lunch pails that they were grateful to eat each day. She explained how the few books and supplies that were available were always secondhand or the throwaway books from the white schools. Then came the stories about integration and *Brown v. Board of Education.*

Mama's history lessons droned on and on as daylight turned to dusk.

During that time, there was a moment when good sense decided to leave my body. I audibly expressed my boredom with an unmistakable sigh. My stupid mistake had barely left my mouth before I saw Mama stand up. She was only five-foot-two, yet she appeared as a giant towering over me. Her voice turned from stern and sad to angry and disappointed. "It is unfortunate that I am boring you. Perhaps you will think more of this conversation when we return to your school to speak with your teacher. If you deserve another spanking, I will be happy to oblige you and see that you get one there—and, if needed, here again at home. Meanwhile, I have many tasks planned to help you positively reflect on this situation. You are restricted from playing outside until I see a positive and permanent change in your attitude. You will come home with satisfactory grades in deportment and no less than a B in all of your academic subjects. And you will be an indentured servant for any elderly person in our neighborhood who needs help with household tasks or grocery shopping. In short, for at least a month, you will spend all of your waking hours working hard and cheerfully at school, working hard and cheerfully at home, and working hard and cheerfully as a volunteer in the community. You, my dear, have just taken fun and play out of your schedule for a very long time."

Mama began to walk straight shouldered and defiant from the kitchen. I was relieved. At least the verbal beating was over; however, that tongue-lashing was nothing compared to her disappointment in me.

She was almost through the door when she stopped in the middle of her stride. "One more thing," she returned to say, "as long as you are black—and that is a mighty long time—don't you ever disrespect the honor of those whose shoulders you stand on. You must never forget the sacrifices others made so that you could live with freedoms and advantages they never knew. You must always remember that with these freedoms come responsibilities—and a commitment to excellence."

She left the room. I got up to leave as she rallied back to the kitchen for one last shot. Gently touching my shoulder, she whispered, "Excellence is always something you should expect of yourself. Your signature is on everything you think and say and do."

In strange and wonderful ways, that punishment was a blessing. I had ample time to get a brand-new attitude. I also had time to learn about myself through the service to others. Most of all, I had time to fully understand the value of education and experiential learning—precious gifts that keep on giving.

SERVICE

How do you serve when need is apparent
and direction is not?
Just see with your heart and begin.

———

Plan service into your schedule—
just like you do everything else.

———

Some of the most powerful people
simply do great things quietly.

A MOUTHFUL OF PRAISE

*A*s children, my sister and brother and I felt that we were in church during most of our waking hours. There was always some program or activity going on, and Mama claimed there was always service to be done at church that was just right for each of us. When I came of age to decide how I would serve, I chose the choir as my just-right activity.

I loved to sing. I loved to hear Mama sing and harmonize. I loved to hear others sing as well. In Sunday school we had been taught to speak loud—in a proud fashion. We were told that it pleased God when we shouted our praise. That sat well with me as I was prepared to sing with full-lung capacity and vigor as a cardholding member of the youth choir.

I walked into my first choral rehearsal with the pomp and circumstance of someone in charge. With one of my better dresses on and some borrowed dime-store perfume, you couldn't tell me that I wasn't the cat's meow.

All the songs we rehearsed were well known in our household. I smiled as we sang each spiritual, hymn, and gospel song. I knew all the music and lyrics so well I simply closed my eyes and tried my best to fill the room with the joy of hearing myself sing. I got so involved that I missed a few directorial cues. *No worry,* I thought. *I'll just keep my eyes open more during the next rehearsal and pay better attention.*

As rehearsal ended, I gathered my things and moved in the direction of our choir leader. I wanted to thank him for allowing me to be in the group. Before I could speak, however, he spoke. He stated that he was glad I stayed behind to speak with him because he had something he needed to say to me as well. My heart was racing. Had he noticed my enthusiasm? Did he recognize my vocal ability? Was he going to ask me to sing a solo? My excitement could hardly be contained.

Standing over me, he abruptly proclaimed, "Olga, you are too loud and too unorthodox with your singing to be in this choir. You sing with abandon and too much passion for the other voices to be heard." His somber presence grew larger and larger. "You did not pay attention, and you wailed more than you sang." He took a breath and administered his last devastating blow. "This is a Methodist Church. We don't whoop and holler. You need to find a place in the church where you can fit in better." My youth choir ministry came and went in a flash.

I was shocked. What kind of Christian servant would kick an eleven-year-old out of the children's choir on the first day? Why couldn't he work with me and help me not to praise so loudly? Who was he to say I couldn't sing? My anger turned into tears as I walked away from rehearsal and waited on the church steps for my mother to take me home. All I wanted to do was praise God. This wasn't right.

It took forever for Mama to pick me up. As I waited, I overheard someone speaking about the usher board—the church greeters. I recalled how they stood tall in the aisles every Sunday and walked with dignity. They were uniformed, white-gloved, and authoritative. I liked their style and grace. They gave orders—and I certainly liked giving orders to folks. But I still wanted to sing.

As I mulled over my options about service in the church, an "angel usher" seemed to step in to save me. A longtime member of this organization found me sitting on the steps outside and stopped to greet me and talk with me about my day. She sat with me and listened with kindness to my sad story about being "fired" from the choir. She spoke quietly and honestly about service and about finding a ministry in the church that was just right for me. Then she invited me to join the youth usher board.

Just as this gracious soul finished comforting me, Mama drove up. She waved, and I went running as the "angel" disappeared before I could turn back to thank her. On the drive home, Mama and I discussed my day and my duty to serve in the church. She explained that my talk with the usher was no accident. She encouraged me to join the usher board and serve without fanfare or recognition—quietly and gratefully. She helped me understand that service in the church and community was an obligation and a privilege—an act of spiritual thanksgiving.

That next year I joined the junior usher board. The adult leadership in that group helped me to become confident as they expertly trained me to meet and greet with hospitality and a servant's heart each person who entered the church. I found my service niche in my church community, and my voice took flight in new directions after that. Mama never stopped reminding me that service opportunities are growth opportunities—always available, always needed, and always apparent if I am willing to keep my mind open and my heart humble.

AUTHENTICITY

How grand is the knowledge
that God made each one of us
uniquely special.

—

In your life walk,
play your own music,
sing your own songs,
be your own person.

—

You will pay a high price
for charting your own course.
The cost is worth it.

IN SEARCH OF ME

When you're a teenager, certain truths start jumping out at you. One fact was certain: I was never going to win a beauty contest. In high school it was particularly painful to live in the same house with the stunning beauty of my sister and then go to class with a majority of young women who could walk off the pages of any fashion magazine.

Hard as it was, however, I did not hide; I found refuge in the forensics and debate team. In the safe harbor of words, I discovered amazingly wonderful friends. These friends were not concerned about makeup or social bravado. These friends only welcomed my need to understand more, to travel further in my mind. They were companions of hope. Little did I know I was soon to be tested.

It was our greatest challenge to date—the much anticipated high school forensics festival at Trinity University in San Antonio. Competition would be fierce, and I would need every advantage I could get! Should I wear makeup? Should I change my hairstyle to something more exciting or dignified? Should I borrow a suit or work overtime to buy one? Or would one of my favorite Sunday-go-to-meeting dresses be best? All kinds of questions obscured my clarity and understanding about myself. After days of private struggle, I went to Mama for advice.

She listened to my saga. After a "hmmmm," she looked into my eyes and spoke the following words with razor-sharp intensity: "Beauty is merely a perception. Conceive yourself—and your art of words—as beautiful. Believe it to be true. Act on that belief by being your best self!" This message was all I needed to move forward.

On the day of competition, in pure joy I gave every part of me. I survived each round of poetry and made it to the finals. Just before the last round of competition, Mama's reassurance echoed in my mind: "Conceive yourself and your words as beautiful." As I began reciting during the last scheduled performance, I found myself being transformed, lifted up by the heartbeat in each word I read. There seemed to be a connecting bridge from the author's heart to mine. I experienced an excitement I had never known! Abandoning my concern about audience understanding and acceptance, I closed my eyes and bathed in the richness of the poetic song.

As the final round ended, my exhaustion hit me. Physically, mentally, and emotionally, I was drained. I had taken every word that belonged to another writer and transformed it into my personal message of hope. I had given wings to Mama's belief in me. What could have been just a simple oral interpretation assignment emerged as a love song and lifelong lesson about the power of language and its ability to connect with our better selves.

My coach encouraged me to rest until it was time to attend the awards banquet that evening. I decided to go home and refresh myself. After all, the banquet was hours away—and win, lose, or draw, I would be happy with the outcome. I had found a new place inside of me that was open to giving and receiving grace and love. In my mind I was already a winner.

Daylight crept toward nightfall as I made my way home. Three bus rides later I found myself walking through the front door of the house, where Mama was waiting to hear how I had "sung my own song." Too tired to eat dinner after our chat, I asked to be excused. A sweet weariness accompanied me to bed for a prebanquet nap.

Next thing I knew my mother was awakening me the following morning with news that I'd had a visitor the evening before. My forensics coach had been concerned about me when I didn't attend the awards ceremony, and Mama hadn't wanted to wake me from what was obviously a deep and sweet sleep. "She left something for you," Mama said. "You need to get up and see what it is."

Since all the important things were always left on the dining room table, I dragged my body out of bed to find an unexpected gift positioned center stage. A first-place trophy. Attached was a notice of a one-year scholarship to the prestigious Trinity University.

More beautiful than the trophy and scholarship was the deep inner knowledge of found treasure—the power and beauty of words. "You are an artist," Mama said as we admired the trophy together. "Artists work with their minds and hearts and bodies…and you did that. It is your words—the poetry of your everyday words—that make you an artist. Keep letting your words and your voice be so fine that they feed the senses."

Artist…me! How rich and sweet were Mama's words to my senses!

INTEGRITY

Underneath our clothes,
we are all naked as jaybirds.

—◆—

You can't outrun a lie.
It will always catch up with you.

—◆—

Your best bet in life is
to try to be as honest as possible
to that person who greets you
in the mirror every day.

PAYING THE PRICE

I was solemn as I approached Mama. As far as I was concerned, the decision had been made.

"Mom, I would rather catch three buses and leave two hours earlier for school than pay for a thirty-minute ride to campus."

Mama seemed taken aback. She quickly responded, "I thought the ride situation was working out for you. We're spending a little more money for convenience, but you get there without having to worry about the weather or the buses being on time to make your connections." Mama had tried so hard to make the trip to my new high school easier for me. She believed that sharing a cramped car ride with three other classmates was a better alternative to suffering three long bus rides and unpredictable weather. She was also concerned about all the transfers from bus to bus in the darkness of early morning and late nights. Frankly, none of that bothered me because I loved the solitude and the newness of each day's darkness and all of the characters who came with it. This was rich text for a wannabe writer. Bus-stop communities have their own special way of teaching you about life and protecting you from harm.

Knowing full well that I could not avoid a discussion, I was ready with my defense: "It was a great idea initially. It's just that the car trip seems even longer than the multiple bus rides. The conversation is always about clothes and money and the right labels and perfumes. Or about guys and other people's business that I have no interest in whatsoever. I just feel uncomfortable. I get this sick feeling inside of me when I hear certain things. And sometimes when the talk is about other people, I wonder, *What do they say about me when I'm not around, especially since I'm not on the list of the most popular or rich and famous?* Let's face it, Mama. I am on the debate team. To most people that means dull and boring. And the people I hang around with at school are artists, creatives; that's not cool either. I just don't *fit* in that car crowd."

As I heard myself speak, I watched Mama's reactions. I knew I had to be more convincing. "Anyway, I have nothing to contribute to the conversation," I continued. "I don't even *want* to contribute to the conversation!" I paused to evaluate my message again. I wanted my mother to know what I felt without explaining everything or sounding apologetic. "Mom, we don't have the money to buy expensive clothes and shoes and perfumes and jewelry. And even if we had money, I wouldn't spend it on that!"

I didn't know whether to allow Mama time to ponder my message or to go on talking. I wanted her to understand, but I didn't want her to question what I knew to be true in my heart. For good measure I added, "You taught us to be neat and clean and respectful…to work hard and treat people as we want to be treated. You instilled in us an attitude of excellence that has nothing to do with where we live or what we buy or who we know. The simple fact is that those girls want to be who they are and I want to be who I am—and none of us seems to want to change, nor should we. Their interests are not my interests."

My tone went from mild frustration to a wonderful sweet peace as I concluded. "I don't mind paying the price to be myself…even if it means that I'm a loner. So be it."

Mama had been listening intently. Finally she said, "When anything you do doesn't feel right, it usually isn't." Touching my shoulder firmly with affirmation, she added the following precious words that still echo in my innermost being: "I trust your judgment."

A fine feeling sets up housekeeping in your soul when you know you have made decisions that are true to you and good for you. I'll never forget that strong "grown-up" moment and Mama's blessing.

DISCRIMINATION

Every living being has the same blood...
and it all runs red.

—❦—

Ignorance seeks the company of humans
in every color.

—❦—

You cannot speak for everyone in your race;
you speak only for yourself.

AND I HAD TO OPEN
MY BIG MOUTH

*I*t was the early seventies, and I could feel that college diploma close at hand. Graduation was a hop, skip, and a jump away. I prayed that no one and nothing would get in my way. I was oh so ready.

It had been a long struggle, a crazy flying-on-faith struggle. When I wasn't at work, I was taking classes. When I was out of class, I was studying or trying to sleep for a couple of hours. I might as well have entered a convent for all the social life I had. But I kept reminding myself that I wasn't there for a social life. I was there to get an education as quickly and as economically as I could. My determination was unwavering as I pursued my degree. In retrospect, I entered college as a young adult; I came out of my institution of higher education as a full-grown woman with a no-trespassing sign in full view.

Just before graduation, I experienced a defining moment. One of my professors asked me to come to his office for a conference. As I made my way to his department and his little corner of the world, I wondered why he needed to talk to me. I knew I was passing his course, and I certainly didn't make trouble in class. With over one hundred students in class, I was surprised he knew I existed. He never called my name aloud or the name of anyone else. He just came to class and read his notes and lectured. He never initiated personal conversation with students. Why in the world did he want to see me?

In my heart I hoped I was wrong, but I had a sickening feeling in the pit of my stomach. It was that same feeling I had as a supporter of the civil rights movement…when trouble loomed. Was it possible that this meeting had something to do with my being the only person of color in class? I wanted to be wrong.

I greeted the professor as I entered his office and stood until he told me to have a seat. There was no conversation for almost three minutes while he appeared to be searching for something on his desk.

At last, notes in hand, he began speaking of concerns he had about "people like me"—colored people, Negro people, Nigra people. He wanted to know what we were calling ourselves these days since the civil rights movement. I wanted to answer, "People…we call ourselves people and human beings." But he never stopped talking long enough for me to answer. Instead he continued his monologue about why we—"you people"—were making such a big fuss over issues of equality and opportunity. He insisted that our behavior would lead to no good, that we should just stop while we were ahead and let sleeping dogs lie. He went on to explain that today we were far better off than our ancestors who were slaves. Weren't we grateful for all of the progress? Why couldn't we be satisfied and grateful with the current situation?

I must tell you, it was a speechless moment—and I have very

few of those! I was saddened and dismayed as I continued to half-heartedly listen and drift away in my thoughts. I sat there thinking, *How in the world did this so-called educated man even begin to assume I was the spokesperson for my race?*

The ghosts of discrimination began stamping through my memory. My first day of school in a new neighborhood… Mama had decided (as a tax-paying citizen) it was only right that her children go to a nonintegrated school around the corner instead of being bused across town to the nearest colored school. My classmates couldn't take their eyes off me, and one of them finally blurted out, "She's colored!" Having grown up in a neighborhood where different races, classes, and religions were represented, I never thought about race until that moment. I was six years old.

Then there were the times I was told I was unworthy of employment because I was an African American. The time I was hired for a job after a telephone interview and later dismissed when I reported to duty and my employer instantly discovered I was black. An occasion when someone threw urine on me and a stranger spit on me because my color wasn't pleasing to them. The memories of marches and sit-ins, boycotts and bus rides. All of it coming back with a vengeance. *Lord, what should I do and say?*

As I floated back to the professor's monologue, his final question shocked me into rapt attention. He leaned across the desk and asked with all sincerity, "Tell me…just what do you people want?"

"Who people?" I asked. I had already chosen to forget the earlier "you people" part of his one-sided conversation.

He looked surprised and indignant. "You people…colored

people, Nigras, Negroes—whatever you call yourselves these days! Just what do you want?"

It was one of those "Mama moments." One of those times when I needed to pack just a few important words into a powerful, meaningful message. I needed a show-stopping Mamaism to end this meeting. *Olga,* I said to myself, *you need to think before you open your mouth and insert your foot! Push aside the negative feelings and take care of the task at hand. Remember who you are and whose you are. You can be strong, respectful, and truthful. Think, Sistah Girl, think. And stay cool. Stay cool.*

"Sir, I can't speak for everyone in my race. But I'm pretty sure I have the right answer to your question or at least one answer that will put this concern of yours to rest. First, I need your help. I need you to do something for me so I can give you my best answer."

He became curious and anxious as I pulled paper and my best pen from my book bag and placed them on the desk in front of him. "I need you to make a list of all the things you want in life," I confidently instructed.

"Right now?" the professor questioned.

"Yes sir, now. Right now." I intently watched him write the list and consider his answers as if taking a test. I began gathering my things.

"How long a list do you want me to make?" he questioned.

I stood up. "As long a list as you desire, sir. Take as much time as you need. And when you get to the end of it—when you finish thinking of all the things you want for yourself in life—just sign my name at the bottom."

All those years of practicing good posture with a book on top of my head finally paid off in that moment. I walked out of my teacher's office as if I owned the place. Walked tall from that office into a larger world with the deeply ingrained knowledge that my blood runs red—just like everyone else's, Mama had said. Like every one of God's children.

MARRIAGE

When you find the right person for you,
your heartstrings demand attention.

—◆—

Opposites attract...
and that makes for plenty of excitement.

—◆—

Total acceptance does not mean
total agreement.

THE CONNECTION

*W*hen I saw him, there was a connection. Something so phenomenal…so strangely exciting and mesmerizing. Who was he? As he sat alone on that piano bench at my friend's house, his very presence seemed to beckon. I decided it was my personal duty to introduce myself and welcome him to the party.

Understand this: When you are fifteen and one of Mama's female children, you do not date, do not wear silk stockings, and do not wander off anywhere without a group. (This was the old "safety in numbers" rule.) All of Mama's children also had names, addresses, and phone numbers of every host, and money tucked away so we could call home if we found ourselves in a situation where escape was our best option.

Escape was the furthest thing from my mind. The mystery man looked like Smokey Robinson. I soon found out he was nineteen and on his way to Vietnam. Quiet, reflective, kind spirited, well mannered. My heart was gone in a New York minute.

I did not know when we would meet again after that night. I just knew we would. And we did…thanks be to God. That mystery man, Clinton Davis, became my husband.

Marriage…husband. The sound of those realities was wonderful, fine, and frightening at the same time. What did I know about marriage or being a wife? Nothing. In the past when I wanted to discuss the "m" word with Mama, it was a short conversation—and she didn't mince words: "You don't need to be thinking about marriage until you finish your college education. And when that time comes, you'll have enough sense to know who will be the right person to marry. Just don't go looking for anyone… Meet your future husband naturally on life's pathway."

That time had come. At age twenty-five, I was married and committed to a relationship with someone I dearly loved whose background was different from mine. I needed advice. As I broached the topic with Mama, she sat still awhile before she offered her words of wisdom. "Marriage is a journey like no other. At every twist and turn, there is a surprise, a challenge, a joy, or a hurt. There is adjustment and learning if you choose to grow. There is forgiveness, hope, and tenderness when you least expect it. It is hard work and good work—but *work* nonetheless if two individuals are to survive successfully as one against the odds."

She walked to the bookshelf and brought back two of her treasured volumes. She pushed the first book gently in my direction. "Just as the Bible is your basic foundation in your past life, so it is in your new life. I know you have your own Bible, but now you need a family Bible as well. Start by reading 1 Corinthians 13. Then continue reading other Scripture passages daily. All the guidelines you'll ever need for your marriage are in the Bible." She then pushed another volume my way. "Keep *The Prophet* by Kahlil Gibran handy as well. His message on love is simple and profound. Each reading will bring new insight."

Mama had assigned the homework. The rest was up to me. I remained quite certain I was still ignorant about this new life I had chosen. Could I really learn what I needed to know from any book, even the Bible? I knew the "instructions" were there, but would I understand how to follow them?

Suddenly my mind was filled with memories of Mama's walk as a married woman. My inside smile became deep and wide. From a very young age, and throughout the subsequent years, I had heard friend and foe alike say that Mama was good for Daddy. She helped him become a better husband, father, and friend. She had been so strong, so surefooted, so elegant in her love, faith, and hope. Knowing this was more reassuring than anything she said that day. Mama's personal marriage model was the manual I needed...and an example well worth following.

SPONTANEITY

Moments can be magical if you're willing
to be spontaneous with your joy.

—·—

When kindness is spontaneous,
it takes on a life of its own.

—·—

Do something new and spontaneous
every day.
It keeps boredom at bay.

GOING FOR IT

*M*ama had spontaneity running through her veins. I believe she was born with it. She certainly had it full tilt in her fifties.

I, on the other hand, tended to struggle with genuine spontaneity. For me, an activity had to be planned and mapped out and considered a few different ways before I could be comfortable with the idea of doing something new. Mama, with the aid of my husband, decided I needed a "makeover" in spontaneity, and they were determined to seize the moment that holiday season.

It was New Year's Eve 1979 when Clinton told Mama and me to dress in formal attire and be ready to have a good time. I had no idea what he had planned, and I was a bit apprehensive about going out on New Year's Eve when we had always stayed home. Not Mama! Her enthusiasm, along with Clinton's, overrode my reticence. I knew if I did not go willingly I would be left behind to see in the new decade by myself.

My husband looked absolutely stunning in his tuxedo as we set out. Mama and I weren't half bad either in our lovely long dresses and coats. Off Clinton whisked us to the Officers' Club for an evening of dining, dancing, music, and laughter. Hats, horns, ribbons, and bells adorned every table. A live band was playing music of every style—user-friendly to those without rhythm as well as those with experienced dancing feet. A glass wall offered the perfect view for fireworks lighting up a pitch-black sky of random twinkling stars. As Clinton danced with me, we had big fun pretending we were some of the best movers and shakers on the floor. Then he tried to coax Mama to cut a rug with him. At first she insisted she would much prefer to watch us work out on the dance floor, but Clinton quickly devised a plan she couldn't resist. The three of us would dance the remaining tunes together!

On the slow dances, we swayed together in a threesome. On the fast dances, we individually did our creative movements in a small circle of quick-moving feet. We were a sight to see—or so people told us. As the evening came to a close, Clinton, Mama, and I were the only "young folks" on the floor. We applauded and cheered the band as they reciprocated with one final tune. Again we applauded and then sang the last song together as we danced.

In the middle of it all, Mama decided to execute a solo dance. She twirled, waved her arms, and put on her best Lena Horne and Ginger Rogers act. She cut her own rug and was tickled with herself. We were so pleased to see her having such a good time.

After it was all over, we thanked our musical friends again and headed back to our table to gather our belongings. The band leader came over and complimented Mama on her dancing. I'm not sure if he was flirting with her or just being generous with his praise. Whatever the case, the end result was delightful as Mama blushed and enthusiastically verbalized her appreciation. In all my years of childhood and adulthood, I had never noticed my beautiful, dark-skinned mother blush. It was like watching a lovely orchid expand and shine.

In the forty minutes it took to reach her home, Mama was silent in the back seat of the car. We thought she might be dozing since she wasn't giving directions on how to drive. As I looked back at her, however, I saw she was fully awake, gazing out the window. After we parked in her driveway, Clinton came around the car to help her out and walk her to the door. Meanwhile I turned around to kiss her and thank her for coming with us. To my surprise, I saw she had tears in her eyes. It was then I realized just what a great time she'd had—and just how long it had been since she had dressed up in formal clothes, gone dancing, and had such freewheeling fun. I noticed Clinton had tears in his eyes too as he returned to our vehicle. He realized this had been a magical evening for each of us—and one of the best times in Mama's adult life.

Each time I remember that night it becomes a wide-smile memory I am fortunate enough to relive over and over and over again. Mama was naturally open to newness and adventure—ready to go for it as long as she could. What a great quality to have, to exhibit, to share.

And me? I'm no fool. I always try to pay attention when someone gives me a gift. I knew that the best thank-you I could give Mama was to try to develop an open mind and heart—to go for it too whenever the magic of spontaneity called my name.

SELF-ESTEEM

Loving yourself is lifetime work.

———

*The art of loving yourself
is laughing at yourself…
and accepting your truly best efforts
as good enough.*

———

*Sometimes you have to leave
the person, place, or thing you love the most
in order to save yourself.*

PRECIOUS CREATION

*I*n our childhood home a sign hung high on one of our back walls:

> *God first,*
> *others second,*
> *self last.*

I never questioned the meaning of that epigram until I found myself lost on a dark path of misunderstanding.

At one of my job sites, I had worked diligently on a project for many months—no overtime pay or compensatory time was offered. It was not the first time I had overextended myself as a "volunteer" on a worthwhile effort to benefit others, but this time the project had taken a serious toll on my family and personal time. I expected nothing but the forward movement of a proposal that would successfully generate many thousands of dollars of scholarship monies for our students.

None of that happened. My work was stolen, and another person's name was applied to my creation. I was distraught and angry. All I could think about was that sign: God first, others second, self last. *What good was it to pray and work hard and treat people right when crucifixion was the end result?* I decided to share my sad tale with my mother.

Mama shook her head and stared at me as she sat down at the kitchen table. "What makes you think life is fair?" she started. "And what gave you the impression that you shouldn't love yourself at least as much as you love others? Let me tell you something, Sistah Girl. Life is a journey that demands all you've got—and then some. Better take care of yourself and keep your senses about you. Better love yourself enough not to allow others to dig a grave for you and then happily push you in!"

I didn't say anything. I knew she was right. I just sat there, still as a corpse, hoping she wouldn't slap me up side the head with another string of famous last words. As luck would have it, she heard me thinking. Obviously my thoughts were so loud I might as well have declared, "Incoming!" Mama just gave me that "look."

She stood up, stretched, and started tending to whatever task she had at hand that day. "Oh, by the way, darling dear…" She smiled and paused. "Do your work joyfully without expectation of credit or recognition. Do the best you can, and do it without regret. Learn when to say no and when to say yes. And never give anyone permission to steal your joy. Love yourself a whole lot more than that."

I stood up, pushed the chair under the table, and commenced my exit. There was a hush of anticipation in the air. I knew she would have one more thing to say before I left the room.

"One more thing…" She giggled. Caught! My escape wasn't fast enough. "Yes, just one more thing I have to say about all this." I turned to face her. "I believe it is an insult to God when you don't completely love his precious creations," she announced. "And it's probably the worst insult of all for you not to consider yourself as such."

Precious creations! Each of us is God's precious creation. Maybe if I had approached the project at work with this truth in mind, I would have seen myself in the positive light I needed—and seen the inestimable value of others at the same time.

"Precious creation." Sometimes you have to hear your rightful name from someone else before you can truly begin to acknowledge it…and later claim it and act out of it.

SECURITY

Never depend on others for your security.

———

*Whatever security you think you have
isn't a certainty.*

———

*Overconfidence is an open invitation
to danger.*

THE LIONS' DEN

Several months had passed since I had been verbally attacked by a member of the church leadership in a public meeting. It was unexpected and shocking. I found myself unable to respond to an erroneous assumption about my service.

First stage: shock, denial, and numbness. It hurt to be betrayed by a group of people I thought respected me and the community mission we had been assigned by our pastor. Was their behavior connected to my twenty-year junior status? Did my thinly veiled irritation after two and a half hours of group indecision and negativity upset them so much that they turned on me?

Second stage: fear, anger, depression. Clearly I had ownership for some of the problem. So I stepped up and admitted my confusion about the disorganization and time-management issues. Bad move. These comments spurred another insult; I was dismissed and referred to another leader, who was trained in counseling and who later betrayed my confidence about a personal matter.

Following that incident, when I attended church, I avoided the persons involved. I still felt uncomfortable months later. I wanted to get all these matters cleared up, but I kept being dismissed by members of the leadership team. "Let sleeping dogs lie," I was told.

Knowing I was a long way from understanding, acceptance, and moving ahead, I finally asked Mama for advice. First I gave her my opinion—and refrained from filling her in on any of the details of the situation. "I'm thinking that maybe I need more prayer to move past the loss I experienced in what I thought was a secure place."

"Were other people in this secure place?" she asked innocently.

"Well, yes," I replied.

Mama smiled as she busied her hands with chopping fresh vegetables. "Then there was no way this place you are talking about was 100 percent secure. That's not realistic. And you're not realistic if you think anyone or anyplace or anything will be completely secure all the time." She paused and put her hand to her chin. "When I find myself in different situations—especially when it comes to my service in the church and interaction with others—I try to remember Daniel's plight in the lions' den. He thought God had forsaken him. God let him know that he had not promised Daniel wouldn't have any trouble in his life. What he did promise was that he would be with Daniel always...each step of the way." Mama resumed working as she continued talking. "Just remember to keep God at the center of your heart and situation. Only if you do that will all of this make sense in the by-and-by."

I wondered if I had truly kept God in the center of this project. Or had I been looking to the people in my group for recognition and appreciation and a secure sense of belonging? Where was my heart of service in all of this?

Even though I never told Mama the specifics about the incident at church, she managed to have the answers I needed. My service in the church or the community had to be without an "I" agenda. Over the years she had browbeaten us about remembering that the least important word was *I* and the most important word was *we*. Now Mama knew what I needed to hear about where to place my trust and focus without knowing the particulars of my problem. She knew the way that mamas just know.

TRIBULATION

Hallelujah for troubled waters!
That's when you really find out
how well you can swim!

When ill will comes your way,
don't always try to outrun it;
sometimes it's best to just sit still
and cover up.

Learn to laugh at your troubles.
That way you will be cheerful
most of the time.

CHANGING COURSE

When an old friend invited me for a visit and to accompany him to an event, I saw the opportunity as a win-win-win situation. I could network, see an old friend, and possibly advance my career. It was going to happen on "foreign soil," a faraway city with a group of people I didn't know; nevertheless this chance to improve my professional position overpowered a smaller, stiller voice within that told me to stay home and make the best of my current situation.

From the very beginning of the trip, disturbance dogged my steps. At the airport, an anxious and hurried departure was followed by the longest flight I have ever taken. After I arrived at the hotel, there was a major miscommunication at the reception desk; I was lucky to get a room. At the first group encounter with my professional colleagues, I was met with barely civilized interrogation. At the main event, at dinner, and at the after-dinner party, I got the unspoken message loud and clear: "We couldn't care less about you."

How naive I had been! Here I had been thinking I was a wanted guest and a potential candidate for collaborative work; the powers that be had no such intention. This group was convinced I should move from the fresh-meat category to an unmarked grave.

No sooner had I sized up the situation than Mama's words came to mind: "When discomfort knocks at your door, pay immediate attention. Then learn the lesson and, if necessary, be ready to change direction. And for heaven's sake, when you are run over by an eighteen-wheeler, don't lie there and wait for the enemy to back up and run over you again!"

I felt myself begin to relax inside, and I started to smile as I tuned out the critical and ostracizing voices around me. I was ready to change the direction of this speeding train. A simple, invaluable lesson recorded itself on my soul: I should have listened to that still, small inner voice in the first place. It is always a reliable beacon, revealing the right direction.

No more time to stand on the tracks in the dark. I immediately found the nearest telephone to arrange for the earliest flight home the next morning. After gracious good-nights to my friend and our hosts, I put the day's tribulations behind me and retired to bed—both humbler and wiser.

FAITH

Faith is leaping out into an abyss
with the full knowledge
that you'll eventually land on your feet
in a dance position.

—◆—

It takes courage to fly your faith
when ground travel seems so much safer.

—◆—

Count your many blessings…
calm will eventually settle in.

FLOWERS

*J*ust keep the faith," I heard Mama say in my mind. "Keep the faith."

The words rang through the depths of me as I questioned if what was happening was reality or a dream. Only a few hours earlier Clinton had made a miraculous recovery; his condition had changed from critical-care unconsciousness to animated conversation and joy. His doctors were amazed and awed; they couldn't explain it. I remember thinking how powerful prayer is—and how soon we might be leaving the hospital together and going home. Euphoria took hold of me at the thought of resuming our lives.

Now his breathing was again labored and frightening. We were again put on a waiting list for the intensive care unit.

The hours passed slowly as we waited and I prayed. "Keep the faith," I mumbled over and over. Maybe our wonderful doctor would work with God to achieve another miraculous recovery. I again pleaded with God again to let my dear husband and friend live.

The night lasted forever. At daybreak we were still waiting. I looked at my watch in time to discover I could make it to the morning worship service. That inside voice screamed at me to go to the service. Believing that God would not let Clinton deteriorate further while I was gone, I hurried downstairs to the chapel.

As God would have it, the chaplain spoke about faith and read one of Clinton's favorite Bible passages. "Keep the faith," I recited to myself throughout the service. "Only God knows the plan."

Returning to Clinton's hospital room, I found him struggling weakly for breath. Frantic, I called the nurse again about the transfer to ICU. She reported there was still no room. I felt like screaming so someone would be forced to come help him...but the sound never escaped my throat. Inside the trembling began as I moved to the window to repeat my faith mantra.

I could see that it was going to be a beautiful day. I closed my eyes, and a twilight calm washed over me. *Everything is going to be all right,* I thought. When I opened my eyes again, I noticed Clinton's breathing had changed. It was easier...more peaceful. "Thank you, Father!" I whispered as I turned again to look out the window.

A few minutes later my husband's easy breathing turned silent. Had Clinton slipped away from me while I looked away in faith? I was tormented by the thought.

In our talk later, Mama claimed that wasn't the case at all. "You walked with him in faith until your last moment on earth together," she said. "Aren't you grateful you were there to take the walk? And aren't you glad his suffering is over? He really is all right now. Everything is going to be all right."

I could not be comforted. And I was overwhelmed with anger. I started crying again and commenced babbling about all the bouquets of flowers Clinton had given me and Mama and his aunts and the sick and shut-ins. Yet in the earthly room he inhabited during his last days, we were not allowed to bring him flowers because the space was needed for medical equipment. Flowers…all I could think about when I saw his face in my mind was flowers. How he loved them and loved to give them.

I didn't realize Mama was still in the room. Her gentle voice washed over me like a balm. "God likes flowers in his kingdom too, darling. And Clinton was one of the most beautiful flowers of all."

When the storms of life rage and mangle our dreams, it is difficult to feel grateful. Yet, all along I have known that God has been so good to me. I had a husband-friend I adored…and one of God's greatest gifts was to be there with him to the end.

Understanding the truth of what Mama told me gives me comfort while my heart continues to ache. Meanwhile, I keep the faith.

WORSHIP

*We can rejoice in the Lord
anywhere, anytime,
with anyone of like heart.*

———

*You get to lay your burdens down
for a while
when you worship.*

———

*Can't help but feel better
after a good church service.*

COMMUNION

*M*ama loved a good old-fashioned worship service. She grew up as a PK—preacher's kid—and was required to attend those dawn-to-dusk services where you dressed up for God in your best Sunday-go-to-meeting clothes. All day they would kneel deep, bow low, and passionately lay their burdens down. She said that spirits moved like winds from all directions in their church as courage music, hope music, love music, and faith music soared to the rafters. Because she wanted the same spiritual education for her children, we went to Sunday school and church every week until we were grown enough to leave her house and make our own way. Yet whenever we were home, worshiping together was a given.

Mama never missed her churchgoing unless there was an emergency. That emergency arrived as a combination of illnesses ravaged her body and forced her to stay in bed. She was especially sad that the illness had been prolonged so she would have to miss Communion Sunday, always celebrated on the first Sunday of the month. Television church services had helped her make peace with forced absences, but now that the first Sunday was upon her, the substitute media options just didn't replace her church experience.

Improvisation was one of a multitude of art forms Mama taught us. Since the minister had not visited Mama in weeks, why couldn't we prepare a communion service for her? After all, she had always proclaimed, "Worship can happen anywhere and anytime…wherever two or more of us gather in his name." I decided then and there that Mama was going to have a good old-fashioned church service with her daughters on that first Sunday of the month.

As I prepared the tray of bread and wine, I considered her favorite hymns. We would sing all the verses of "Amazing Grace" and "Just As I Am" and have an order of service just like the one on first Sunday. The tray was ready; the hymnal was under my arm. I made my way to Mama's room where my sister was waiting.

"Mama, we are going to have our own Communion Sunday worship service. Here. Now. Scripture, psalter, prayer, songs, and the Lord's Supper."

At first she looked shocked as the information registered. She sat up in the bed. "Is Reverend coming to give me communion?" she asked.

"No," I replied. "I am your minister of communion today. You taught us about the priesthood of all believers—that each one of us is a minister of God. I am acting on that today, knowing he will guide me in this gesture of love and remembrance."

Mama was too weary to argue. The service began. It was short and sweet in content but overflowing with warmth and wellness, blessed by God's grace. Although Mama never expressed feeling better, she seemed to look better. One thing was sure: I got to lay my burdens down for a while.

The next day, after not hearing from the pastor for five long weeks, he came by to give Mama communion. My sister told him that I had already given Mama communion. Then she politely thanked him and bid him farewell. To hear her tell it, the look of shock on his face was a genuine Kodak moment.

When Mama returned to church, the pastor politely questioned my authority to give communion. Mama smiled sweetly and replied, "Gestures of love are always appropriate, don't you think? Anywhere and everywhere we gather in his name, we can be ministers of the Master." Another Kodak moment arrived as our pastor walked away without saying a word.

I have that title: minister of the Master. It is a gift I try to honor daily.

RECEIVING

There are many great ways
to do small things
for the people you love.

— —

Learn to appreciate your loved ones
before it's too late.

— —

Never forget that love
is a noun and a verb—
both at the same time.

THE GIFT

*C*ousin Rodney had promised to come see my mother. Every time he had planned to come in the past, his supervisor had issued one of those surprise assignments, and Rodney had canceled. You could hear homesickness in his voice. When he could finally come to spend just a few hours of his free time, he hurriedly got in his vehicle after a grueling week of twelve-hour workdays and very little sleep and drove over two hundred miles to be with Mama.

What joy in his sharing! He is the kind of person who lights up a room with confidence, cheerfulness, and wild but wise abandon. We exhausted ourselves with laughter from the moment he arrived until he had to leave less than five hours later. His every verbal and nonverbal gesture demonstrated his great love for his Aunt Browning. And she loved him at least as much.

After showering him with additional love and affection, we waved good-bye until we could see Rodney's Jeep no longer. Mama sat down on the porch and became quiet. She looked perplexed and very concerned.

"Why the long face?" I asked her. "We have had an exceptionally glorious day. What could possibly be wrong?"

She hesitated to speak her piece. "Rodney was so tired. He

should not have driven all this distance just to visit me. He should have stayed home and rested. I would have understood."

"Yes, you would have understood. But he wanted and needed the gift of your presence, Mama. It was more important to him than sleep or rest or play or anything else."

She was irritated by my homily. "It is dangerous for anyone to drive when he is that tired. He did not *need* to make that journey."

As soon as she uttered that last sentence, I could sense her recognizing a deeper truth. I, nevertheless, spoke it aloud: "It was part of the gift, Mama…the journey was part of the gift." I watched Mama's frame visibly relax as she received it.

I've thought of that moment many times since, when I've felt myself resisting what those who love me have tried to give. "There is no greater gift than the gift of one's true self; there is no better thank-you than a welcome of appreciation," I remember Mama chiming throughout the years. "Receiving, too, is an art form."

Mama was right…right as rain.

REGRETS

You can't always UNdo what you did;
next time just do the right thing
to begin with.

— —

You can learn a lot
from other people's mistakes.

— —

Can't do a thing about yesterday.
Don't know if tomorrow will come.
So work with today.

PUTTING OUT THE TRASH

"When will you get over it?" I heard myself asking her. Hearing the scolding tone in my voice, I took a breath before I continued. "Mother, you did the best you knew how at that moment in time…and that was good enough. You need to learn the lesson, then put this situation in the trash where it belongs and leave it there."

I was beyond irritation. She was regretting yesterdays when she couldn't help her grown children in ways that only they could help themselves. "There is never any failure when you do your best for God. Anyway, it is over…over. You couldn't bring back yesterday if they gave you all the lottery money or Kentucky Derby winnings!" She had to smile at that remark. We both remembered her pastor's sermon about all the sinners who played the numbers…how they should be giving that money to the church instead of gambling. In fact, as far as he was concerned, state lotteries and gambling trips were just plain sinful. The good reverend spent over thirty minutes on this pet peeve one Sunday—too long for Browning's liking. At the end of the service, she politely asked him if he would mind if she gave a sizable portion of her lottery winnings to the church. He thought it was a good idea.

"I know you are right," Mama sighed. Not wanting to dwell on how right I was, she turned the tables on me. "I remember a time when you regretted an action you took—or didn't take. I know it's human to make mistakes. And I know that sometimes you didn't want help from me when you were in a fix. I had to acknowledge that fact and then move on and just pray for you. I know all these things. But I still have some regrets."

The next second I heard myself take a Mama-like breath and spew a full-scale sermon in her direction. "So if you 'know all these things,' then act accordingly! Give it to God and *leave it there*." The words continued forcefully out of my mouth. "Everything you did, you did with a loving heart. You can browbeat yourself all day and all night about shoulda, oughta, coulda, woulda. You didn't! So get over it, all right?"

The silence was deafening. Maybe I had overstepped my bounds. Oh well, I was still breathing. Might as well go for the kill. "Now it is time to grant yourself permission to forgive yourself for a sin you never purposely committed. It's over!"

More silence. Realizing that maybe a quick exit was the best recourse, I got up to leave. She headed me off at the door, and her embrace came before I could read her face or eyes. "How did you get to be so wise?" she whispered.

I hugged back and replied, "Maybe the apple doesn't fall far from the tree."

ATTITUDE

*You are not allowed to bring any negativity
into this household...
just leave it at the curb.*

—◆—

*Attitude—more than the gray matter
between your ears—determines your success.*

—◆—

*Who in their right mind
wants to keep company with a sourpuss?*

STARTING OVER

*F*unny how your attitude can color an entire day. I had made every effort to plan a positive day: a four o'clock rising, prayer and meditation, Scripture reading, journal writing, exercise, breakfast and vitamins, shower, and the outfit of the day ready to go with plenty of time to spare. As I navigated the car out of the garage, however, the day began changing course.

First, the flat tire. No problem—a call to road service. An hour and a half later, there was still time to get to work on schedule. Caught in rush-hour traffic, I practiced breathing exercises to keep my cool. As the cars inched along slowly, I decided it might be better to stop at a convenience store and use the phone to alert my supervisor about the traffic and my situation. No answer and no working voice mail in her office. My frustration level began to spike. As I left the store, a kind soul who had overheard my mumbled conversation with myself extended a cup of coffee to me and suggested I take a detour. I accepted the coffee and the advice and boldly steered my vehicle into traffic again. Before I inched ahead even one mile, a young driver cut in front of me. As I abruptly braked to avoid a collision, coffee suddenly and artfully decorated my outfit. Home again I went to change clothes and to try again to call my boss. Still no answer.

I eventually arrived at work three hours after I'd initially left my house. Before I turned the key in my office door, I was met by angry students and colleagues who all wanted to know where I had been and what had happened. I let them talk at one time until they got tired of outtalking each other and realized I had not responded. Only then did I say, "And good morning to you, too!" A hush fell over the group long enough for me to set my belongings down and catch my breath. Then one by one, I honored their concerns.

It didn't get better as the day progressed. In fact, it got worse. New and unforeseen tasks had put on magical tennis shoes and found their way to my desk—tasks that were due for completion yesterday and yet had appeared just today. There was a meeting to attend where the egos in charge indicated clearly they would not be assuaged unless everyone agreed their opinions were gospel. And there was another two-hour mandatory meeting to look forward to—only this gathering was to ask for input about decisions that had long been secretly written in stone. I was mentally, physically, and spiritually exhausted…and it was only two o'clock in the afternoon.

Any other time most of the nonsense wouldn't have fazed me. But today was fraught with madness. And my attitude at this point was just plain ol' bad.

On top of everything else, I had a graduate class to attend in another county. Stopping to grab a bite to eat before I tackled the highway, I looked at the menu with dissatisfaction. *Breathe,* I said to myself. *There is something on this menu that appeals to you. Look closely and breathe.* As I tried to center myself, my eyes closed for what seemed like forever. When I opened them again, a waitress was standing over me with a perplexed expression on her face.

"Are you all right?" she inquired.

"I will be as soon as I get something to eat," I barked as I continued eying the food fare before me. She assured me that she would return shortly. Meanwhile, I stopped to evaluate my behavior. Why had I been curt with the waitress? She didn't have anything to do with my challenging day. She was innocent. When she returned, I quickly apologized and ordered breakfast.

"Are you sure you want breakfast at this time of day?" she queried. "It's after three o'clock in the afternoon."

"Yes, dear, I am sure I want breakfast," I replied as I handed her the menu. "I want to start this day all over again."

She walked away shaking her head. I moved to the telephone booth, remembering that I had forgotten to call Mama that morning. It was a ritual with us to speak early in the morning.

After I told her my tale of woe, she said, "Be grateful to be alive to start your day all over again. Only this time, make sure you have a good attitude—no matter what comes your way…'cause a bad attitude will kill you quicker than a speeding bullet."

I enjoyed my afternoon breakfast and got on my way to class. There was a brand-new day before me, and I had a chance to color it with the right attitude.

PREPARATION

*Pitiful preparation
makes for poor performance.*

———

Preparation never takes a vacation.

———

*If opportunity knocks at your door
and you aren't prepared,
just pretend that you know
what you're doing.*

THE TRUNK OF MAMA'S CAR

*B*eing a child of the Great Depression, Mama always believed that you had to be prepared for anything and everything. Being a preacher's child, she was also willing and able to preach you a sermon on the topic.

Mama was compelled to give me one of those sermons when I continued being tardy for my first class at school. "You are slow as molasses! The only way you can correct this tardiness problem is to be better prepared."

I turned a deaf ear. The fifth-grade social and academic work was hard enough. The last thing I wanted to do was get to school any earlier.

"Are you listening to me?" Mama demanded.

"Yes ma'am," I quickly responded.

"How will you be ready for opportunities that come your way if you are not prepared?" Mama questioned. "Opportunity doesn't just keep coming back to you and pleading for a chance. You have to be physically, mentally, and spiritually prepared. School helps you become mentally prepared for many of life's challenges." She was obligated then to highlight exactly how her brothers and sisters prepared for school when she was a child. Then she talked about how they walked miles to school in every kind of weather. She followed with how they ate nourishing food from their gardens and preserved and canned excess crops to prepare to stay healthy. She proudly noted that each child in her family worked in the community and at home from sunup to sundown. As if that wasn't enough, she wanted me to know that most of the clothes they wore were handmade. "All of it was about preparation," Mama concluded. "Remember: Pitiful preparation makes for poor performance. Do you want to be labeled like that?"

"No ma'am," was my short and wise answer. The less I said, the better my chances to move on to a different topic.

Now, more than forty years later, I remember that conversation as if it happened yesterday. Understand this: All my life Mama has carried essential and interesting items inside the trunk of every car she has owned. "I always want to be prepared," is her explanation. Water, snacks, paper towels or rags, an ax, and a few other things I dare not mention were always in the trunk of the car. I could understand hauling around some extra rations for the body. The paper towels and rags I could also understand; emergencies happen. But the ax? That was beyond my comprehension. After years of traveling with her, I needed to know why Mama insisted on carrying an ax in the trunk of her car. So I got up the nerve to ask her. "What does an ax have to do with preparation?"

"Why not an ax?" she retorted defiantly. "You never know when you might need to give something—or someone—a good whack! Always be prepared. Always." Not a peep from me. That was the absolute end of that conversation.

What has not come to an end is the topic of preparation. Just yesterday Mama was saying that you should be prepared to act as though you are prepared even if you don't know manure from Muzak. "And if you act like you know what you're doing long enough," Mama said, "pretty soon you will be able to figure out a way to do it."

Sounds like a plan to me.

WORK

Let your work be your passion…
only then will you never go hungry.

—❦—

Your work becomes a masterpiece
only when you use the whole you—
your head, your hands, and your heart.

—❦—

Work at doing your best work;
work harder at being the best you.

NANNY AND PAPA'S
LEGACY

*W*hen my maternal grandmother and grandfather were considering retirement from pastoral ministry, Mama was still gracefully struggling with working, raising a family, supporting the well-being of the children in our community, serving the church, and committing us to a host of learning and extracurricular activities to ensure that we were productive, well-rounded Christian people. When my grandparents did retire from their ministry in the Methodist church, they came to share our home.

Our grandparents were the incarnation of a strong work ethic. As Nanny raised chickens and built pens for them in the backyard, Papa transformed part of that yard into a vegetable garden overnight. Each tool they used had to be immaculately cleaned before the work was finished. Their system for working was efficient and economical. When we needed something, the first consideration was if we could make it ourselves. Buying things was the last resort.

I am my grandparents' granddaughter. Physical work offers me a cleansing—a renewal and a step back in time to appreciate the discipline of work. So it is that with a yard three times as big as my house, it sometimes feels like a demented type of therapy when I decide to mow, trim, and plant in this space.

Once, after many spring rains, the grass had grown very tall and willowy. I started with the weed eater and kept whacking that grass until the equipment started smoking. Realizing this was not a good sign, I disconnected the machine and began raking up the damage. Not five minutes later the rake came apart—not once, but three times. I declared aloud, "I shall not be defeated!" After finding some wire and creating a new-and-improved tool of unusual artistic design, I called it a day. My body was weary with the good feeling that comes from great effort—but it was proclaiming, "No more!" Tomorrow I would start again with my Nanny and Papa's spirit in tow.

The next day the weed eater would not start at all. I decided to borrow Mama's sickle until I could figure out what to do. That sickle was an old, tried-and-true weapon of destruction. It wasn't until I came home with it and poised myself for the first full swing that I realized its unique structure. There was a screw missing; it, too, had been wired together in a uniquely artistic way.

Mama was her parents' daughter. Neither of us had spoken about the broken tools—much less had we thought about throwing the damaged equipment away! We both knew there had to be a way to make these old tools work to our satisfaction. In spirit and action, we had a can-do attitude.

Nanny and Papa modeled the internal joy of personal accomplishment for both Mama and me. Somehow my grandparents managed to love the work of their hands so much that the chickens and produce gave up all their secrets. The freshness and tastiness of the eggs, tomatoes, squash, okra, and beans were as important as their appearance. My grandparents left us a legacy of love for work and plants and nature. No matter how poorly Nanny or Papa was feeling, they would return from the yard or garden renewed.

The same way Mama does. The same way I do.

LEARNING

Learning is forever.

———

True learning requires sharing.

———

*Anything you want or need
to learn about
is in your Bible or the library.*

ABRACADABRA

*A*ll I wanted to do was fulfill my commitment to my students and have our annual spring theater season. The administration declared there was no money that year for our tradition. Being Mama's child, I had to find a way to keep that promise to my community.

When I told my tale of woe to Mama, she didn't have any suggestions about how to find the money. She did have a speech though. "You are already spending too much of your own money for the plays at school. I know that administration hasn't reimbursed you in the past for monies spent, so don't expect them to do it now. Two things are for sure. First, you cannot afford to keep on using your money for this type of endeavor. Second, I am as sure as I am black that you have the ability to figure out a viable solution."

"Like what?" I cried out. "I need the money they promised me and my students to make this happen." Anger was setting in. "All they have to do is take some of their entertainment or travel funds to help us out this season. We have a proven track record, a full house of community members and students for every performance. If necessary, we can charge for tickets and pay our own way next season."

"You are preaching to the choir, Sistah Girl. Have you tried going to the president? It won't hurt to ask."

So I went to the president of the college and asked for help. I was determined. Our conversation didn't last long. He explained that the biggest expense was acquiring amateur acting rights for the plays my students performed. "If it weren't for that expense, we could have a theatrical season," he confirmed.

I felt myself puffing up as I promptly announced the problem was solved. "I will just write a play myself," was my answer. "Then we won't need to worry about the cost of any rights." He grinned, nodded his head, and dismissed me—probably as incapable as well as unbelievable. I thanked him and left his office full of myself. Once outside his door and in the hallway, I braced myself against the doorjamb and slid down the wall. What did I know about writing a play?!

At home Mama was waiting for me, eager to hear the news. When I told her how my ego and big mouth had taken over the conversation, she, too, grinned and nodded her head. Did she also doubt I could fulfill such a promise? Before another negative thought could enter my head, she reassured me. "You can do anything you want to do if you are willing to keep learning. The fact that you love your work and love to share it with others makes you ripe for a new season of self-education and development. And the fact that anything you want or need to learn about is in your Bible or the library is evidence that the resources are available. Abracadabra, my dear. Abracadabra!" Mama's eyes twinkled.

"Abracadabra?" I asked, impatience coloring my tone. "What in the world does that have to do with anything?"

"It is a word associated with magic. You have the magic of your mind and spirit. I have been told by an African friend that it is also a word of encouragement from ancient souls; it means 'hurl your mighty thunderbolt'!"

I don't know if Mama conjured all that abracadabra foolishness or not. I only know that she gave me the message about learning that I needed to hear. After weeks of my going to the library with my Bible, after prayer, reading, and study, an original play was born.

With a successful opening season behind us, Mama and I found ourselves replaying all the obstacles that had brought us to that victory. She shouted aloud, "Learning is forever! Thanks be to God. Isn't that wonderful?"

Yes, it is, Mama. It truly is.

LISTENING

Give a full hearing.
Listen to the line between the lines.

—◆—

God gave you two ears and one mouth
so you could listen more than you speak.

—◆—

You don't always have to have the last word.

MONOLOGUE PEOPLE

*I*n every family you have at least one. Maybe more than that. They are the people who love to hear themselves talk. You could put a blindfold over their eyes and leave the room; they would just keep right on talking and never miss you. When they call you on the telephone, you could actually put the telephone down, complete a few tasks, and return; they would never miss you. The only important thing to them is their agenda.

Most times you try hard to tolerate them. Sometimes, to no avail, you try to interrupt them and change the direction from verbal monopoly to inclusive dialogue. Occasionally you try to disagree or add your two bits, which is an automatic invitation for serious debate. Other times you accept the situation, excuse yourself, and allow others the opportunity to be held captive. Such was the case at a particular family gathering when my patience was wearing thin. After listening as long as I could, I left Mama to fend for herself with our family talker.

Now Mama is one of those people who rarely misses an opportunity to let you know how she feels about the topic at hand. In a nice way she tells you in no uncertain terms what she is thinking, especially when you get on her last good nerve. Without a doubt our family talker was doing just that. However, much to my surprise, she said nothing after being held captive for over an hour. Unbelievable! Was this the same Mama who invited me to go home as soon as I completed her honey-do lists…the same Mama who didn't want to waste endless conversation about things she couldn't do anything about? Who was this woman sitting and listening to the droning of a self-focused monologue? It had been a one-man show for over an hour, and she was still listening. Now she was shooing me away so she could listen some more. I decided to stay, watch, and honor her attentiveness. It was mesmerizing.

On our way home from the gathering, I felt the need to address my bafflement. "Mama, sometimes I don't understand your actions at all. I cannot believe that you sat and listened to that monologue without getting a word in edgewise. Had that been me on a verbal rampage, you would have called it to a halt."

She responded promptly, with a note of mischief in her voice, "A: That wasn't you. B: Had it been you, I probably would have nipped it in the bud. C: You would have understood why I needed to cut you off."

For some reason her frank remarks did not help my aggravation. "How can you be so patient and tolerant with that kind of selfish behavior?" Hearing the irritation in my voice, I changed the tone and direction of the conversation before Mama could engage (I thought). "Anyway," I concluded, "for the most part, I know that you were not actually paying attention. There were a couple of times when you took a nap!"

"How do you know I was napping?" she snapped.

"I think it was the light snoring or the bobbing and weaving of your head that helped me come to that conclusion," I retorted. "Really, Mom, you have the patience of Job. I know you were bored out of your mind with that one-sided conversation. You've told me numerous times how nerve-racking those 'sharing sessions' are. So why did you encourage that behavior?"

"Well," she began, "this time it was different. This time I needed to listen. He was in pain. I heard his pain more this time than ever before. So I decided to listen as best I could in the hope that he would hear himself. I know I could have interrupted him or given advice, but I didn't because I knew he would not have heard me. I just listened and silently prayed for him with the hope that he might discover his own answers after hearing his voice in the universe."

We rode the rest of the way to Mama's house in thoughtful silence. After our usual "I love you's" and hugs, she left me with a benediction. "Sometimes you have to stop and listen with your heart. Sometimes a person's pain is more important than your inconvenience."

Mama has always had a natural way of helping people see with new eyes. Her wise words about listening encouraged me to create a better script for dealing with monologue people. And I know that listening with my heart is an art form that needs constant attention and improvement.

SELF-CARE

*A worn-out body can never successfully carry
a weary soul.*

———

*When your soul is weary,
learn to ask loved ones
for the important gifts:
acceptance, love, and prayer.*

———

*It takes courage and determination
to choose life—not death.*

A NEW SCRIPT

*M*ama was sick again. Weak as water. She had not taken care of her basic needs before she took care of family members, friends, and any other someone in need of help. Why did she have so much trouble practicing the basic concept of healthy self-care? She had told me herself, more than once, "You can't take care of the world before you first take care of yourself."

She quietly rested for a few days at my home as I plied her with hearty meals and gave her a hiatus from the telephone, meetings, and errand running. During that time of care, I was on slow boil. Only when I saw her color coming back and heard her taking on a feisty tone of voice did I seize the moment to let her know exactly how I felt.

"Tell me, Mom, when you try to save the world, is it a woman thing or just a Mama thing?"

"It's my thing!" she snapped. She was taken aback by my question, yet I could tell by her tone of voice that she was feeling more like her old self.

"Well, dear, 'your thing' isn't working very well." I took her food tray back to the kitchen. Before I could start washing the dishes, she was standing in the doorway with her hand on her hip.

"Are you upset with me?" she asked.

"Yes, I am." I struggled to keep a civil tone. "I want you to be well. I want *you* to want to be well so you can do all the things you want to do." I was determined to give her some of her own medicine. "I remember you telling me when I was young, 'When you consider your own needs, include everyone else.' But haven't you taken that a bit too far lately? You are doing a fine job of considering everyone else, but look where it's gotten you! Your 'script' ain't working. Shouldn't you rewrite it to say, 'Take care of your own basic needs first and then serve others'?"

Mama bristled. "You are taking what I said out of context. When you were young and demonstrating selfish behavior, I tried to remind you that your needs weren't necessarily a necessity for everyone else. When you wanted possessions that you didn't need to sustain you—and that I could not afford to buy—I would say, 'If it is not a matter of life or death, you don't really need it.' And, yes, I did say, 'When you consider your needs, include everyone else.' A family unit has to think about each family member. You can't just go off like a crazy person and consider only yourself and your needs."

As strong as her words sounded, I could tell that Mama was unsteady on her feet. I took her hand and led her back to bed. I hated to see her suffer, and I knew she hated not being able to take care of herself.

She positioned herself on the pillows and had the rest of her say. "As much as you want to do this for me, you can't. I'm the only one who can make *me* my first priority. You simply cannot be in control of my well-being. It is my responsibility to take care of my own needs." Mama's yawn was a message to leave the room. "We'll talk about this another time," she said sleepily. Then she mumbled something about "Invictus."

"Invictus"? Wasn't that the poem by William Ernest Henley? The poem she loved and had to memorize for her seventh-grade teacher? I called the library in a determined attempt to find that work as soon as possible. Once located, I hurried to check out a copy. These lines were powerful and timely. I hoped Mama would be pleased and inspired.

After she woke up from her nap, I read "Invictus" to her. Then I paraphrased the last two lines: "You are the captain of your fate...the master of your soul." In the ensuing silence I wondered what she was thinking. Would this strong mama of mine try harder to take better care of herself or simply dismiss my concern with the familiar "When it's my time to go, it's my time to go" line?

"Maybe I do need to think about how to rewrite this 'needs' script of mine," she finally said.

Progress, I thought. *We made some progress.* Even a little progress is good.

In the days to come, Mama actually took her own advice. She began walking again and forcing herself to eat well. Fruit replaced candy and cookie treats, and broiled fish and chicken substituted for fried food. She began feeling better and looking better; the glow came back to her cheeks and a kick found its way back into her step. She was truly working at being well for the first time in a very long time.

Mama wasted no time making sure I heard all the details of her efforts to improve her health. She was excited about her progress and hopeful about her future again. I listened intently as she explained her plans for rejuvenation and renewal. At times she would repeat aspects of her regimen that were most important to her. When she did, I knew these were points she wanted me to "get" myself.

"Did I tell you about all the miles I walked today at the park?" she would say in her authoritative schoolteacher voice.

"Yes ma'am, you did," was my studious reply. Mama being mama, I wouldn't be surprised if in the very near future she required me to take a test on everything she said about good self-care. Woe on me if I fail to pass that test!

PLAY

*There is a child's heart
that lives in every human.
Keep it alive!*

———

*Do not worry about whether or not
the sun will rise;
just be prepared to enjoy it.*

———

A family needs to pray and play together.

A FUN CHALLENGE

*M*ama had never been to the Laity Lodge women's fall retreat. When I invited her to go with me, she was excited. "You get to come play with me," I said, the delight evident in my voice.

"I hope you have the energy to keep up with me," she replied.

Laity Lodge has been and continues to be a spirit, mind, and body Christian renewal center for the weary, the worn, and the wandering. This Eden in the Texas Hill Country is a retreat where learning, growing, sharing, and unconditional acceptance are givens. If you need to rest, you do so, with the only interruption being the mealtime bells to remind you to eat. And if you choose to eat, homemade Mama food awaits you. In this safe, uplifting, and joyful place, you blossom—even if you elect to be a thorn.

Once at the lodge, Mama was like a child in a candy store. She was in awe of the breathtaking scenery, state-of-the-art facilities, and outstanding hospitality from everyone she met. She wanted to attend every event, identify every species of plant and bird, visit every adjoining camp, and go with the "young folks" on every hike. I was worn out just looking at her bounce from one thing to another.

On our drive home, Mama was exhausted but talkative. "I love to play," she confessed. "When we were children, we had little time to play—we were always working. But when we were allowed to play, we played hard for as long as we could. I felt like a child again at Laity Lodge."

"Play looked good on you this weekend," I confirmed.

We went another thirty miles before she said anything more. "I want to keep my child's heart alive. I want to play more often," Mama determined. "And *you* need to play more often too, Sistah Girl. You should put play in your agenda just like you put work, rest, and service." She began searching through her purse for paper and pen. "So when will you start doing that?"

"As soon as I finish the big project I'm working on at school," I chimed in weakly.

"That is not soon enough." I kept my eyes on the road, but the Mama "look" was palpable beside me. I knew she was waiting for me to come up with a better answer. I said nothing.

"Sometimes we forget that tomorrow is not promised," she continued. "I'm making a note that on this day you committed to putting play in your schedule. And when will that be?"

"As soon as I finish that project," I repeated.

I heard the disappointment in Mama's voice. "Play is not something you should put off until later," she challenged. "The demanding job you have begs for play and rejuvenation. More play time for you is quality time to stoke your creative fires for the project you are working on and all the others to follow."

I knew she was right. I also knew I needed play time more than my job at that moment. Maybe we could help each other commit to having more fun. An idea popped into my head. "Would you consider taking dancing classes with me?" I asked.

"Only if you find me a good-looking, smooth-talking, thirty-something man to glide me across the floor each time we go for a lesson!" she announced. The thought of Mama bossing some man around the dance floor was too much for the imagination. We laughed until we cried.

"Let me work on that, Mama," I choked out between giggles. "Let me have some time to work on that."

TIME

Use it or lose it!

———

Each moment is precious…
each moment a gift.

———

Only now is promised.

A PAINFUL TRANSITION

*M*ama insisted that we attend a social event together. My beloved Clinton's ashes had been scattered only thirteen weeks earlier, and this was my first large-group encounter. Before leaving for the evening's event, I emphasized to Mama my strong desire to leave immediately after the gathering. My plan was to get in and get out of this social situation as quickly as possible and then get to bed early.

As soon as the program ended, I got up and walked directly to the parking lot. Even though I left Mama in a throng of people who all wanted to visit with her, I entertained the thought that maybe she would quickly follow as I believed we had agreed. Forty-five minutes later she glided to the car.

I was pouting when Mama finally arranged herself in the vehicle. She took one look at me and knew. "Are you upset with me?" she asked innocently.

Why bother to answer, I said to myself.

We drove in silence. I wasn't angry at her as much as I was angry with myself for even going out. I had no interest in socializing at this time. Clinton's death had left me raw and quiet.

"Listen, Mom," I began, "I realize I am not good company at

this point in time." I felt myself measuring the words to avoid offending her. "The pain I am experiencing right now is excruciating. I hurt so much that I struggle for breath at times. And try as I may, I have great difficulty being social at obligatory events that honor other people's needs. Time means something very, very different to me now."

A full twenty minutes passed before we spoke again. The external noise of heavy traffic was drowned out by my memories. Multitudes of memories with Clinton. I felt a desperation to spend whatever time I had in ways that worked for me.

Finally I broke the silence. "We should better plan our time together, Mom. I love spending time with you. I just don't enjoy events that do not help me feel better and be better."

Her lightning response was a surprise and a comfort. "I can understand how you feel. We need to pick and choose what we do together. After all," she chuckled, "you are the old person in the group. I need to hang with young folks more!"

Chuckles exploded from both of us. Mama wouldn't bite her lip for anyone. And truth be told, at that time in my life I *was* the old one. I felt old, looked old, acted old. I was impatient, sad, and ready to cry at the drop of a dime. How desperately I wanted to experience joy and the preciousness of each moment again.

"Be patient and faithful," Mama whispered. "Time will once again be your friend."

"One thousand four hundred and forty minutes in every day," I whispered to myself. Once they are gone, they are lost forever. I knew in my heart that I needed to find better ways to celebrate whatever days I had left on earth. Maybe the pain wouldn't have as much space to dig in and grow if I honored moments more.

Mama reached over and patted my arm. "Be patient and faithful," she whispered again. Then her hand went on her hip and her finger started waving as she began the tough love segment of her message. "Meanwhile, thank God for the gift of each moment. Keep thanking him for his gifts by making the best of every situation. You have no time to do anything but the best you can do."

I had the clear impression that if Mama had her way, I wouldn't have any other choice.

GRIEF

Grief sometimes leaves you speechless,
dumb, and blind.
All you can do is pray.

———

Stay centered in your faith;
turn your grief into celebration.

———

Let grief be your teacher—
not your undertaker.

RENEWING AN
OLD FRIENDSHIP

*M*ama and I could not talk about it. Every time she started to recall her "Clinton memories," I would change the subject. I was guarded and did not want to share him with anyone—not even Mama. I felt selfish and ugly.

I truly did not recognize myself. Who was this "other person" shutting out laughter and joy? The fog of loss blinded me in this unfamiliar place called grief. I did not understand. I could not comprehend how I could help others cross over peacefully and not be—and stay—at peace with Clinton's leaving.

I needed my oldest friend to help me through; I had to find a way to bring her home to me. And so I began saying "Yes!" to our reconnection, our private and public oneness. I was ready and hungry for our new ventures, our peaceful and fierce exchanges, and raw emotional meetings in broad daylight or a blues-filled midnight. I needed my writing, my dearest friend. But she would not come.

"You will find your way," Mama told me. "Just don't go off the deep end and do something crazier than usual." She was reading my mind. I felt like I was on the deep end of nothingness each time I put pen to paper and only senselessness emerged. Or nothing at all. The feelings would not come out to help me clear my head. Yet every morning I commenced the four o'clock ritual, begging the words to be born.

It was a slow process to let go and let God work his mighty plan. Even slower to allow Mama to talk about Clinton and to share memories. When that selfish me finally took a hike, I was able to explain to her one day that I now had a full understanding why people wanted to die when they lost their beloved. I pleaded for forgiveness. I petitioned her prayers to help me feel alive again, to find my voice, and to have the strength to honor those we love in my writing.

The next day at four o'clock in the morning, I began the writing ritual again. This time the words came freely, slowing releasing me from the bondage of grief. In my "Letters to Clinton," the curtains of darkness drew back to let light in. The healing began.

When I told Mama the news, she said nothing. In silence, I heard her answered prayers.

PERSPECTIVE

Have a shoot-for-the-moon perspective;
the worst that will happen
is you'll land on a star.

———

Mud isn't necessarily manure...
it's all in your perspective.

———

The grass only appears to be greener
on the other side.

SEEING BEYOND

I noticed brown patches of grass were creeping up all over my lawn. *Time to water and feed,* I thought. As I glanced across the street at one of my neighbor's lawns, I observed how very green and thick each blade of grass seemed to be. As I walked across the street to take a closer look at the grass, I could see clearly that there were small brown patches on that lawn as well.

Perspective. "It's all in the way you see things," Mama would say.

Later that week I spoke with a minister who was wearing a boutonniere on his lapel—the flowers having died long before. My curiosity about the dead flowers overpowered my concentration as we were conversing. My look of puzzlement got his attention. He asked if I was wondering about the dead thing on his suit jacket. "Yes, I am," was my simple answer. He explained that the decrepit buds were full of seeds, which would become lush flowers after they were planted in rich soil. Later that day, he would give a precious seed from his boutonniere to each of his board members to take home and plant—a reminder that one must plant seeds of faith, hope, and love in commitment to God and his kingdom in order to produce a beautiful harvest in the church.

Perspective. "Think giant, be giant…you never know what will happen," Mama would say.

I try to be positive at all times; however, I know that I have much more room for improvement. And I want to improve. So I've recently decided to keep the door open even wider to possibilities. Each morning I start my day with, "Good morning, Holy Spirit! Thank you for all of the good and great things that will happen in my life today."

Perspective. How many times through the years has Mama told me, "If you keep expecting a miracle, your perspective just might change."

Thanks, Mama.

AGING

Old is as old does.

———

Some people live and die...
and some people never live at all.

———

The older you get, the more you act—
and sound—like your MOTHER.

NEVER A STRANGER

*M*ama never meets a stranger. In the grocery store she holds up the line to ask about the cashier's well-being. At the pharmacy everyone knows her, and they all stop being busy to await her inquiries about their lives. In a restaurant she usually doesn't know the wait staff at all, but before she leaves, they know her. Her energy for meeting and greeting people is as endless as her face is ageless.

On one particular restaurant visit, we had the good fortune to have a waiter who was very hospitable and extremely handsome. After Mama acquired information about his background and his ambitions, the waiter smiled, thanked us, and sheepishly retreated to place our order.

"Mama, that young man has probably never had a customer like you. You were all in his business," I teased. "I'm not sure he's coming back."

Mama smiled. "Oh, he'll come back. He might be young, but he's not stupid. He knows my intention is good. He probably just hasn't held a decent conversation with anyone sixty-five or over in a long time—maybe never. I intend to let him know what he's missing. People like me are an experience everyone should have."

"People like you?" I laughed. "You mean youngsters over sixty-five?"

"That's right. People forget that aging is a beautiful thing. I have a library of information in me that needs to be shared. I wish every young person could be assigned an older person. Then maybe our 'libraries' could be recorded and family histories kept intact."

"You won't get an argument from me," I assured her.

We sat quietly for a while and began our people-watching segment of visiting. As it happened, a large group of senior citizens arrived at that moment. I thought, *They are probably all Mama's age or older.* As they were slowly being seated throughout the room, I searched their faces in the hope of discovering who thought themselves to be "old" and who acted as if his or her heart was still young. There were telltale signs in the way they walked, talked, and interacted with one another and the restaurant personnel.

Then my mind switched back to Mama. I could have predicted her refreshing response, but I asked her directly anyway, "How do you feel about aging?"

Mama's eyes sparkled as she answered. "As I have aged, I remain aware of how I can do my part with God to age gracefully. Chronological age is a given—and a blessing if you live to talk about it. I can do nothing about the years that I've accumulated. What I do have a hand in is my biological and psychological age. Biologically, I am forcing myself to be more responsible for monitoring and improving my nutritional concerns, rest, exercise program, and stress management. And I am taking my medicine and trying my best to simplify my life."

She paused to consider the next category. "Psychologically, I am young. I am possibly younger now than I was in my thirties." She leaned closer. "You see, I have picked an age and remained there!" Her giggle was contagious.

At that moment we were interrupted by three of her former students. They hugged and kissed their beloved teacher and spent at least fifteen minutes telling her how she was as ageless as her teachings. Mama was glowing. After they left, I told her how very much I appreciated their comments, how right they were in confirming what a wonderful teacher and ageless beauty she was, is, and will forever be.

The waiter was fast approaching with our order when I decided to end this topic of aging. "Now don't get a big head over all that sweet talk about you," I teased.

Knowing she would have to have the last word, I awaited the next line. "Let me give you a bit of high praise," Mama quipped. "The older you get, the more you're beginning to act and sound just like your mama."

That was a compliment I will surely take to the bank.

DEATH

We die a little every day…
even more reason to do joy to the fullest.

❧

Dead is dead—six feet under
or walking around on two feet.

❧

As long as memory holds,
loved ones never die.

FUNERAL DIRECTIVES

It was a piddling day for both of us, an attempt to practice the FAT theory—file, act, or toss. Browning Louvenia moved slow as a mule about the room, sitting more than walking.

"You be the mother today," she moaned.

"Do I get to whip you if you act up?" I teased, the memory of those peach-tree-switch whippings still fresh, even after forty years.

"I know you are not *that* crazy!" Mama quipped. Belly-button laughter ran like a river from our souls. No matter what, Mama had to have the last word. A smiling quiet ran its course throughout the room. Then Mama began, "When I die…" I braced myself for a conversation I didn't want to have. "I want the whole-hog treatment: wake, funeral, and burial next to your father. And you, Missy, had better make sure that my hair is the way I like it and my makeup is just right."

I felt myself unclench a little inside. This was the first time I could remember being patient and empathetic when Mama brought up the topic of her funeral. My own aging had mellowed and matured me.

Mama continued her monologue. "I want you to call every-one…*everyone*. I want a good turnout. Pull out all the phone books and directories and call until you reach all my friends and acquaintances. Leave no stone unturned. I want the big hooty-ha celebration." She paused. "*Or...I will come back from my grave and have some words with you.*"

No doubt, I thought. *No doubt.*

She put her hand on her hip and continued. "I made a list of my favorite songs and scriptures and who I want to officiate." A long silence. I thought for a moment that the topic of death had passed. Wrong! Minutes later her thoughts erupted into more directives. "Don't forget that I look good in purple. Be sure to put me in purple. Not any purple...not that *dark* purple! You have been around me long enough to get that right."

I couldn't resist it; this was an opportunity to make my own "passing over" wishes known as well. "I want to be cremated," I said. "Better still, I want my body donated to science and a memorial service where people write notes about how our lives touched. Or maybe they will opt to speak about our good times on the planet together. Either way, I want it recorded."

I suddenly realized that a coldness, a stiffness, was beginning to set up housekeeping in this room we were now sharing. A shift in our conversation was needed. "What I really want," I added, "is a dress rehearsal before the real event!" Mama looked at me as if I had lost my mind—again. I continued animatedly. "Yes, ma'am, I want an early funeral where everyone can come and say what they want to say and join in the celebration of my sending forth! This way I can rewrite the service if I need to while I am still alive—before the actual fare-thee-well day."

Mama laughed as she shook her head in confirmation of my madness. Out came the wagging finger. "I don't want any part of it…not one iota of your craziness."

We both smiled. As I moved to take her hands in mine and look into her eyes, I said sweetly, "Mother, we need to get something straight. I will kill you if you die on me!"

Encircled by the warmth of mutual love and unbridled joy, we had full knowledge that day: Death will come when it will come—but for now, this moment was a gift.

ACKNOWLEDGMENTS

Where do I begin? Probably at the beginning. Thanks be to God from whom all blessings flow!

After God comes my mama, Browning Louvenia McKinney Samples. The memories I share with you in this book are a celebration of her life in particular and my life in general. I thank God for you, Mama.

Grateful am I also for my families throughout these United States. Your individual names are too many to list here. Please accept my love and gratitude for the many years you have loved me—in spite of myself. Thank you…thank you.

Even before our father died, Mama was wise and gracious enough to allow other Christian women and men to aid in our development from little humans to bigger humans. Everywhere we went in the immediate and extended community, these surrogate mamas and papas provided watchful eyes, swift action, and little tolerance for misbehavior. They were family members, neighbors, personal friends, teachers, Scout leaders, and even corner merchants. Thank you, surrogate mamas and papas, for being a loving, devoted, and watchful village.

Jacob's Chapel Methodist Church and St. Paul Methodist Church were our spiritual safety nets during our childhood years. The people in these churches took a genuine interest in our holistic development; their teachings enhanced our understanding of both

Christianity and citizenship. Church families, thank you for that needed and most necessary undergirding.

The days spent growing up in San Antonio were full of sunshine and shadows. Diane Sydney Rivers and Billy Hunter knew me "back in the day" and loved me in spite of myself. We all pretended to mature together as we understood each other's battles. Most of all, we stayed faithful to one another during the childhood, adolescent, and adult walk. Only blood stands in the way of our official kinship. Thank you, dear ones, for standing by me throughout many years. We've had some epiphanies that could truly be another book.

When I was responsible enough to journey away from home and into a larger and more adult world, I found pastoral care in higher education through campus ministries. It is easy to get lost in the world, but each time I fell, the loving hearts from these ministries provided a strong foundation for recovery. Thank you, nameless and known ministers, for the safe havens of chapels at Hampton Institute, St. Mary's University, and the University of Texas at Austin.

When St. Philip's College became my academic career home, several people consistently tried to support me. Dorothy Carter Pickett, a retired and celebrated principal and teacher, served as the "Mother Superior" of our campus ministry. She had a magnificent way of bending even persons who were determined to be mean in the right direction. In the meantime her "walk" inspired all of us to be better and do better in all aspects of our lives. Thank you, Dorothy Carter Pickett, for teaching all who would look and listen about unconditional love and for helping us know the work that God intended us to do.

Another faithful friend at St. Philip's College, Mark Barnes, has provided bold collaborative venues for expressing and enhancing my artistic fires. Roy Riner, my "identical twin" and colleague, listened and laughed with me weekday mornings at daybreak. His personal story of courage continues to be a daily testimony of hope. Audrey Mosley, our drama diva and managerial genius, whipped us all into shape as she demonstrated ways to work the system so it wouldn't kill us for doing the right thing. Nan Schreiber, an artist in her own right, was always there with words of inspiration and encouragement. Thank you, Mark, Roy, Audrey, and Nan.

Casey Lieberman and Terry Gay Puckett took me to a new level of artistry as we worked together on local and national literary and visual art projects. Our gallery exhibits remain extraordinary to the many lives we touched. Thank you, Casey and Terry, for your fine artistic vision, your patient hearts, and your ageless, loving comfort as I stumbled through the learning and living processes.

Karen Narvarte and Ellen Shull have a corner on the magic, meaning, and mystery of words. As teachers they shine beacon-bright with profound knowledge of literature and goodness. Thank you, Karen and Ellen, for allowing me to be your proud student and friend.

Pecan Grove Press at St. Mary's University published my first book of poetry and prose. Under the outstanding leadership of Dr. Jackie Dansby Edwards, the award-winning Upward Bound program at St. Mary's University extended me a life raft during a time of ongoing loss. The life lessons were valuable and memorable. Thank you, one and all.

In that same St. Mary's Upward Bound program was Professor Don Edward Davis—master teacher, colleague, brother, and friend. Seven days a week Don worked on behalf of his students; not even his critical health concerns deterred him from his mission to teach and to serve. More than any professor I have ever known, he actually worked at teaching nonstop. The Sunday before he died, he called me from his office where he was waiting for a student to show up for an interview. I will forever hold his teaching model as a loving tribute and appreciate his invitation to be a sister. So thank you, Don. I know heaven is happy to have you. And thank you, Helen and Lester "Dado" Davis, for calling me daughter throughout the years and for keeping me in the family.

On my beloved Clinton's slow, long, and torturous last journey, I was honored to have the wise, loving, and gentle Larry and Jan Waddy by my side. Masters of communication and kindness, they listened to the same angry and loving tales while never holding back on the "toughen up" and "hold on" speeches. They knew when to do what and how to do it…serenely and beautifully. Thank you, Larry and Jan. You have been my mentors, my friends, my neighbors, and my brother and sister.

Rodney Wayne Holden deserves a space of his own. He is a blood relative who also is a friend, nurturer, and youthful inspiration. As a lifelong learner and man of faith, his regal height is nothing in comparison to his tallness in character and love. Any mother would be ever so proud, dear one. Rodney, thank you for believing in me and lifting me up when my faith in myself crashed and burned.

When I was lost in grief's darkness, I became weak as I wallowed in abject poverty of the spirit. God gave me the gift of a community of hearts who rescued me and provided me with space, guidance, and prayers for healing, renewal, and restoration. This community did not ask what they should do; they took direction from God and did it, naturally and honestly. When I cried out, they did not even question my request or dismiss my agony; they just held me close. So it follows that I lovingly extend continuous gratitude to the H. E. Butt Foundation Laity Lodge Retreat Center. The vision statement for the center says it all: "So that God may be glorified and nations come to faith, our vision is to equip believers in Jesus Christ to practice servant leadership as modeled by the Holy Trinity to renew ourselves, families, institutions, and society." Terry Gay Puckett was the first to offer my name as a resource person. Don Murdock, the executive director, was the exemplary leadership model who graciously extended an invitation for me to come and serve. Letha Crouch, Carol Murdock, and Bitsy Rubsamen were my guides through the initial Laity Lodge orientation waters. Each one has become a dear friend. Thank you, one and all.

Shortly after Laity Lodge came into my life, in marched Kathleen Davis Niendorff—a gusty, stately, fun-loving Christian literary agent and lawyer. She helped me claim my voice again—a voice that I felt had died with Clinton a year earlier. I couldn't find my sea legs for the longest time, but with her unbridled joy Kathleen kept pulling me up and pushing me forward. Thank you, dear one.

I am at a loss for words worthy enough to thank Random House for believing in my voice. Over a period of many months, the extraordinary WaterBrook Press professionals graciously laid the foundation for this book with the highest degree of competence and concern. Thank you, Laura Barker, John Hamilton, and a host of others, for providing the rocks on which to lay the groundwork of this book. Thank you, Carol Bartley, for walking with me during those last literary miles, and thank you, Pamela Perry, for all of your efforts to pass the love and passion on. Kudos to all—for who you are and what you do so beautifully.

Finally, an enormous amount of appreciation is sent forth to Traci Mullins of Eclipse Editorial Services. As a book editor and encourager, there is none finer. She graciously and gracefully fine-tuned this book—providing plumed-wing flight for its words and images. My gratitude is deep, wide, and profound. Mama and I embrace you in an unending circle of respect and love, dear Traci.

Humbly and with deep appreciation, I acknowledge that I stand on the shoulders of those who have gone before. This book is a celebration of all who helped make me who I am today.

So, I end where I began...thanks be to God from whom all blessings flow!

MAMAISMS THAT SHAPE OUR LIVES

Use this space to record memories of your own mother's wisdom and her approach to parenting and life.

MAMAISMS THAT SHAPE OUR LIVES